DATE DUE

AUG 16 '80

Y636.1
O   O'Connor, Karen
      Working with horses;
   a roundup of careers

PAW PAW PUBLIC LIBRARY
PAW PAW, MICHIGAN

Working with Horses

A ROUNDUP OF CAREERS

Karen O'Connor

Working with Horses

A ROUNDUP OF CAREERS

Photographs by Kelle Rankin

DODD, MEAD & COMPANY · NEW YORK

ACKNOWLEDGMENTS: Special thanks to my friend and colleague, Melvin Powers, and to all the individuals and organizations whose assistance and experience contributed to the writing of this book.

PHOTOGRAPH CREDITS: Photographs on pages 84, 110, and 111 are courtesy of Jack Sweeney. All other photographs are by Kelle Rankin.

Copyright © 1980 by Karen O'Connor
All rights reserved
No part of this book may be reproduced in any form without permission in writing from the publisher
Printed in the United States of America

1 2 3 4 5 6 7 8 9 10

Library of Congress Cataloging in Publication Data

O'Connor, Karen.
Working with horses.

Includes index.
SUMMARY: An introduction, based on interviews with people in the field, to the various careers available in the horse industry including farrier, wrangler, riding instructor, and veterinarian.
 1. Horse industry—Vocational guidance—Juvenile literature. [1. Horse industry—Vocational guidance.
 2. Vocational guidance] I. Rankin, Kelle.
II. Title.
SF285.25.O25   636.1'0023   79-6636
ISBN 0-396-07812-5

For Erin
with love

Contents

	Foreword by Jud Bender	9
1	Your Future in the Horse Industry	13
2	So You Want to Be a Farrier	19
3	Racetrack Careers	32
4	Horse Show Occupations	47
5	Training Riding Horses and Teaching Young People to Ride	54
6	Training Circus Horses	61
7	Working on a Guest Ranch	72
8	Retail Sales	87
9	Horse Healers and Helpers	92
10	Rodeo Riders	100
11	Breeders	109
12	More Ways to Learn About and Work with Horses	113
	Index	119

Foreword

Do you love horses, want to know more about them, and what is involved in their care? Would you like to find out about the ways to work with them? Are you interested in the careers in the horse industry that are available today?

If so, I recommend with great pleasure, *Working with Horses: A Roundup of Careers*. As far as I know, it is the only book of its kind for young people now available and, consequently, it's long overdue.

The author not only provides up-to-date career information but offers a greater understanding of the problems and joys inherent in the related professions, as well.

From my experience as an airline pilot and a professional horseman and entertainer with my palomino, Jet Western, I know how important it is to select the right career. I'm fortunate in having two professions that I really enjoy. If you, too, love horses and want to spend time learning about them and this growing industry, this book will give you the kind of information you'll need. As you read, you can begin to see which professions, specifically, interest you most, and best fit your individual talents. There is no better way to determine this than to take advantage of the advice of those who know by experience. That is what this book is all about.

Working with Horses is straight from the horse's mouth—well, almost! The true value of this readable book comes from the top professionals in the horse industry. They offer solid advice about the pros and cons in their respective fields. Ms. O'Connor's informative and entertaining interviews give you an opportunity to take advantage of and learn from the experts in the industry—people who have succeeded through practical experience over many years.

It is my privilege to have known, personally, several of them. I have seen the high quality of work of Bill Van Gieson of Calabasas Saddlery, Dr. Robert Miller of Canejo Veterinary Clinic, and rodeo champion, Tom Ferguson. These and all the horsemen and women interviewed are among the very best in their fields.

All over the world, interest in horses is growing by leaps and bounds. And as the author points out, the horse population in the United States has more than doubled in the last twenty years. Those of us who work with horses continuously are well aware of the growing need for qualified men and women within our industry.

None of the people interviewed claims that a career with horses is easy. It is not. However, if you set a goal for yourself, work hard, and follow the suggestions outlined in this book, you will be prepared to enter a fascinating and rewarding profession.

Someone once said, "The outside of a horse is good for the

inside of a man (or woman)." If you are looking for a career in the horse industry, welcome to a wonderful world! And I wish you the best of luck in selecting one that's exactly right for you.

Jud Bender
Camarillo, California

1
Your Future in the Horse Industry

Would you like to show, hunt, or race? Breed, raise, or train horses? Teach riding? Become a rodeo clown? Or work as a stable manager, equine veterinarian, or horse equipment manufacturer?

Whatever career interests you, opportunities are available in every field, because at the present time the horse industry is booming! According to the American Horse Council, "There is a great need for qualified employees in many areas of the industry." However, since most young people seek only the glamour jobs of rider or trainer, many other good positions go unfilled. For example, work is increasing on breeding farms, at racetracks, and at private training stables. There is also a growing demand for women in the horse business. Female jockeys get most of the publicity, but many young women work as hot-walkers, grooms, stall-muckers, and pony girls. Name the job and girls can do it! Even schools of veterinary medicine are acknowledging women in a way they never have before. Females now represent nearly 50 percent of total enrollment.

Another area that has great appeal because of the athletic challenge and skill required is that of riding instructor. As riding events such as dressage, cross-country, and stadium jumping expand, there is a tremendous need for instructors who can teach all three.

Although formal schooling is also important for success in working with horses, most authorities agree that practical in-the-saddle experience is basic. It cannot be learned from books. Therefore, riding, reading, and working or volunteering part-time at a ranch or stable are necessary steps to preparing for your career with horses. People who have the most success as professionals are generally those with plenty of experience around horses from an early age.

"Nothing works like experience. You must work around horses," advises young professional, Janet Stratton, who has ridden and trained a variety of horses, such as American saddlebreeds, hunters, and jumpers, for more than fifteen years.

Janet and young men and women like her agree that nothing can match the pleasure and satisfaction of just being around these strong and highly sensitive animals that have served mankind throughout the ages. In addition to fun and enjoyment, you can also learn patience, tolerance, and perseverance from working with horses.

The Importance of the Horse

For thousands of years, the horse has been one of our most useful animals. In the past, horses have provided a fast and sure means of travel. They carried soldiers into battle and hunters rode them into forest and field. They pulled stagecoaches, covered wagons, and carriages.

In recent times, the car, train, and airplane have replaced the

Standard rig for horse transportation—used in a variety of careers.

horse as means of transportation. But horses will always be well-suited to working and running. And for thousands of people, they provide both work and play.

In the last fifty years, for example, the horse has become a means of sport, art, and play. But it was not until after World War II that the horse industry boomed. People had more money then and more free time to enjoy. Gradually, families began moving out of the city to the country. As a result, there was a return to rural living. Riding clubs appeared, trail rides became popular, and horse shows sprang up in many areas.

Dude and guest ranches formed and riding stables filled their stalls with more horses to meet the growing population of enthusiastic riders.

Cowboy muses on the future of ranch hands.

For many people, breeding, riding, training, and grooming horses became forms of work and fun. To many there is nothing like a leisurely trail ride along a shaded creek or in the mountains, galloping through the desert, the excitement of a rodeo, or the beauty and artistry of hunters and jumpers in show.

No matter how much work is involved, the horse continues to be a source of pleasure and pride. Fans crowd stadiums to watch horse races. And horses entertain us in carnivals, circuses, rodeos, and horse shows. They work hard too, not only as performers, but in fields and pastures, helping cowboys round up cattle.

Today there are close to 10 million horses in the United States. That is more than twice the number of fifteen to twenty years ago. As the horse population grows, opportunities to work with them increase too. Many people will be needed to work with and care for horses. And some will teach adults and children to ride and enjoy them.

To best prepare for a career in the horse industry, Ms. Stratton suggests you begin by taking riding lessons. "If you are athletic and have a good sense of timing, you have a chance. But it takes a lot of determination and hours of riding every day—years to become really good. But like anything you wish to do, you must be willing to spend a lot of time and practice on it."

Many of the jobs presented in this book do not require professional quality riding skill, but a knowledge of horses and the ability to ride and handle them is necessary in most cases.

If you are interested in getting into the horse business, keep the following points in mind as you study the career possibilities in the remaining chapters:

—Narrow your field.
—Know what you want to do.
—Contact schools about training programs.
—Speak to professionals already working in the field.

There is a wide range of jobs available. And if you prepare systematically, you'll find what you're looking for. Experience is necessary, so if you are still in school, look for part-time work at a stable, saddlery shop, private ranch or farm and get as much on-the-job experience as you can. Also, if possible, consider taking riding lessons from a well-qualified instructor and learn all about horses and how to handle them.

The following chapters are based, for the most part, on interviews with people in the various fields. It was not possible to make personal contact in every profession, so I chose those jobs that seemed the most interesting and best known. I hope you will find enough here to get you in the spirit, and to assist you in finding a job that suits your talents and interests. And I hope you have as much fun reading this book as I did in preparing it.

2

So You Want to Be a Farrier

Durie Schultz, a young blacksmith (farrier) in Sylmar, California, agrees with the old adage, "A horse is only as sound as its feet."

"If a horse's feet aren't in excellent shape, the animal is worthless as far as performance is concerned," she says, "and that's what the horse was bred for."

With nearly 10 million horses in the United States today, the art of the farrier or blacksmith is in great demand. There is plenty of work in this field for strong, enthusiastic, and knowledgeable workers. It is an ideal career for anyone who likes using a variety of skills in one job, moving from place to place each day, working outdoors, and who enjoys a good challenge.

The blacksmith shop, however, is no longer the stationary operation it once was. It is now a highly mobile one. Farriers move around from one ranch, house, or farm to another, making several calls a day.

Pete Beckman, for example, has been shoeing horses for twenty-five years. His dad had been a horseshoer in Bluegrass, a small town in Iowa. "As a kid, my friends and I always visited the farms in and near the little towns. At thirteen I got a job at our local country club as a groom. I grubbed stalls and groomed horses for $1.00 a day."

During high school Pete dropped horses in favor of athletics, but then went into the military service and again saw the need for horseshoeing. "I had no intention of becoming a horseshoer, but I was stationed in Hawaii during the war and if I had been able to shoe horses then, I would have really done all right financially."

After the war Pete studied the craft through the veteran's program, and then worked at his profession six or seven months each year until 1954 when he and his family moved to California. People wondered what he was going to do in California. "I'm going to shoe movie stars' horses," Pete quipped. "Little did I believe that would come true," he recalled. But once in California, Pete stopped at the famous Fat Jones' Stable, where many of the major studios leased their horses, asked for work, and wound up shoeing horses for a variety of stars. He worked on Mr. Ed, the famous talking horse, John Wayne's horse, Charlie, those in the "Flicka" series, as well as the horses of Audie Murphy, Hugh O'Brien of "Wyatt Earp," Jim Arness from "Gunsmoke," and Jack Mahoney of the "Range Rider," and many more.

What Does a Farrier Do?

Some farriers still make horseshoes from metal bar stock, shaping and welding in coal- or gas-fired forges with hand tools. Others specialize in reshaping or applying machine-made or "keg" shoes, which are available in a variety of sizes, styles, weights, and material for intended purposes.

Durie Schultz is a farrier by choice. She has no trouble with equal rights.

Pete Beckman, farrier and instructor.

Durie Schultz uses ready-mades. "But I have to make many modifications," she claims. To fit the foot, she shapes the shoe while it's completely cold, or heats it for making unusual changes. Corrective shoeing is another specialty which involves making a special foot appliance by hand for treating injured, deformed, or diseased horses. Each animal may need slightly different weights and balances and this takes time and specific know-how.

Blacksmiths must also have a thorough knowledge and understanding of the anatomy and physiology of the horse, especially the feet and lower legs. Being able to handle a horse well is also important. They are flighty animals and require firm but gentle handling.

Sometimes a farrier will work with a veterinarian also. For this, he or she must be able to read and understand radiographs and be familiar with medical terms in order to talk effectively with the doctor.

Farriers need basic skills in handling the forge and its tools. They use a wide assortment of tools in their work. Most of them are simple hand tools, but their use requires great skill. Sometimes they may have to make a replacement, or design and make a specific tool for a specific job. Some of these tools include measuring devices such as calipers, dividers, and scales. By controlling the amount of fuel or the force of air over the fuel, the farrier heats the metal to a certain temperature in a coal-, oil-, or gas-fired furnace. Tongs are used to remove the object from the forge and to hold it in position on the anvil while the farrier then shapes it with a hammer or rasp. Various tools are used in the shaping process. The hardy, pritchel, flatter, swedge block, and forepunch are a few of them. A bench vise may also be used to hold the material. After the farrier shapes the shoe to the

Pete Beckman uses a wide variety of tools in his work.

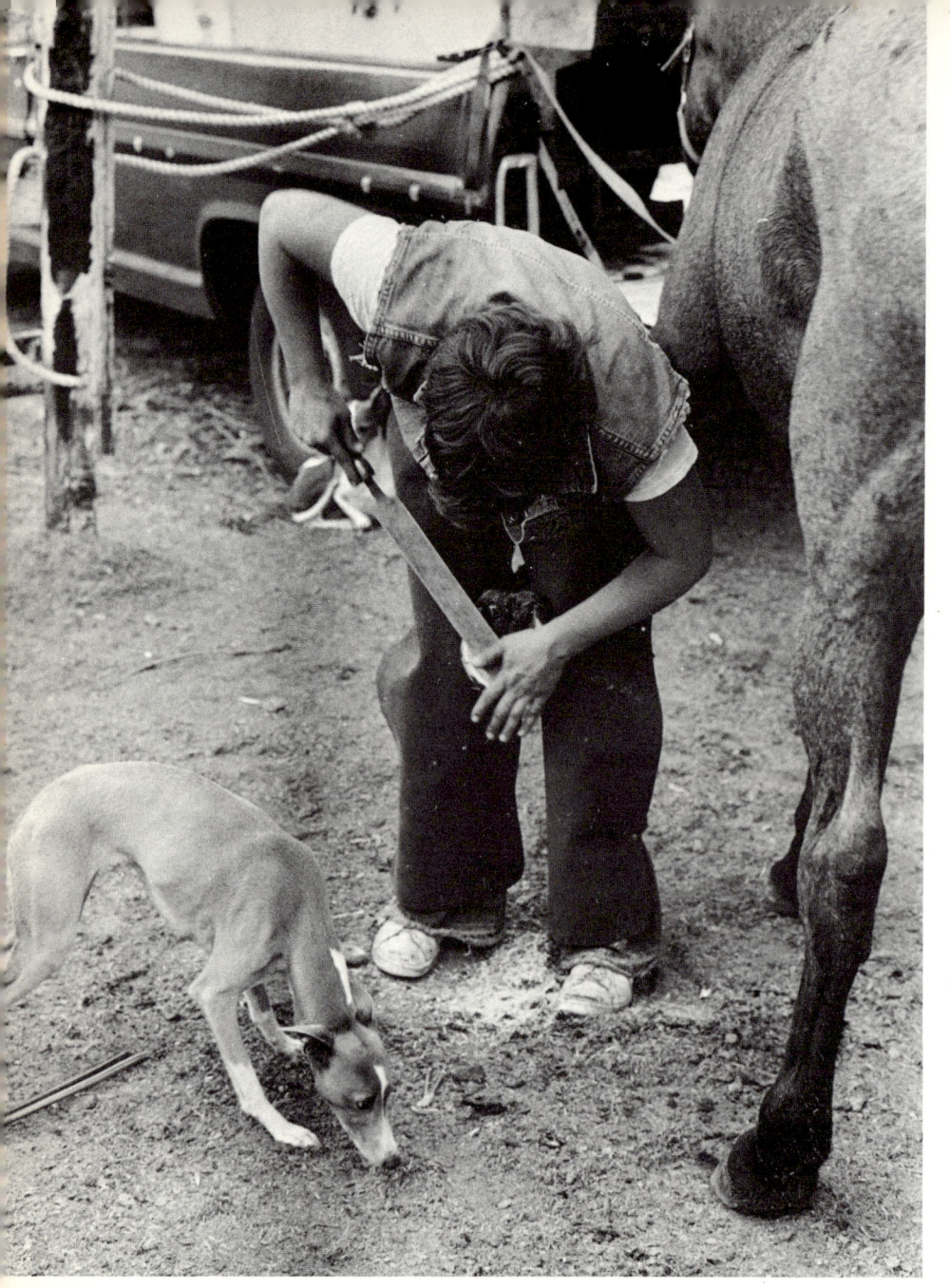
Durie Schultz files horse's hoof while dog carefully supervises.

horse's foot, it may be hardened by tempering it in air, oil, or water. Next, the farrier finishes the shoes by hand with a file or power grinder.

Where Do Farriers Work?

Farriers usually work outdoors in or near stables or corrals. Although most of them love the outdoors, flying insects, odors, dust, and extreme weather often intrude on their work. Sometimes people and passing vehicles also distract them. These interruptions can cause a horse to become flighty and difficult to manage. In these instances a horse can be truly dangerous. Injuries are common in this work, and a farrier must know how to restrain the animal. Cuts, bruises, burns, mashed fingers, and kicks occur often. And there is not much protection other than the farrier's customary leather apron, goggles, and steel-toed shoes.

Durie avoids what she calls *problem* horses—a horse that has anything on his mind besides shoeing. "I usually don't work with them," she said. "It's too risky. There are enough nice animals to handle."

Being a farrier is also physically demanding because the work requires stooping and crouching. Farriers must hold and use hand tools and, at the same time, bend, twist, reach, grip, lift, carry, and sometimes manage a frisky animal.

What Are the Personal Requirements?

Average physical strength, a well-conditioned body, good eyesight, hand-eye coordination, hand and finger dexterity, and a good sense of balance and angles related to the conformation of the horse are important.

Farriers do so much bending in their work that a very tall

person may notice back trouble and in later years find it necessary to give up the profession because of it. Pete Beckman, for example, has some back ailments himself and knows of others who have quit shoeing horses for the same reason. Durie Schultz, however, is 5'5" tall and has been told that she's the perfect height for this work.

In addition to the physical requirements, a basic "feel" for animals is absolutely essential. And this is not generally something you can learn. Skills come with practice and experience but "feel" seems to spring naturally from the individual.

The farrier must also be willing and able to work hard under stressful conditions, and sometimes for long periods of time. These experiences may be difficult for some people but many enjoy the challenge. "I wanted to get into the field because I like to travel and I love the outdoors," says Durie. "I enjoy horses and people, and I don't mind working hard. I prefer this to a desk job. It's a relatively easy profession to get into but you have to be willing to work hard to be successful at it."

What Training and Education Are Required to Become a Farrier?

You can learn to become a farrier by taking formal courses or by observing and practicing with someone already in the field. Durie Schultz recommends that you call people you know or hear about. "Talk to them personally. Listen to what they have to say. Many would welcome an apprentice to hold the animals and to assist with tools and equipment."

In addition to experience, Durie suggests you read everything you can on the subject. "I read zillions of books, mostly veterinary manuals. So I guess you could refer to a competent farrier as an equine podiatrist," she quipped. "Unless one knows as much as possible about the hoof, from the medical standpoint, you can't deal with related problems."

Both Pete and Durie agree that there is no substitute for being around horses. Firsthand practice gives you an opportunity to learn the basic skills as well as how to handle and restrain a horse. For the more complicated studies, which include the anatomy and physiology of the animals, you can attend classes at one of the several "Horseshoeing Schools" operating throughout North America.

During formal schooling, you'll learn basic skills from lectures, demonstration, and actual performance. You'll learn how to use tools properly, how to handle animals, animal psychology, public relations, professional image, business management, and anatomy and physiology of the horse. Completing the course, however, does not necessarily make one a competent farrier. "If you finish the work, they give you a certificate. But that doesn't mean you're a farrier. It just means you went through the course," says Durie. "Someone who hasn't been to school could actually be more professional just through experience."

Although Pete Beckman loves his work and wants to stay in the trade for many more years, he cautions young people that, "It's a long drawn-out process. This profession takes many hours and a lot of devotion to get to where you can make a good living at it." At the present time Pete teaches classes in horseshoeing at the North Valley Occupational Center in the San Fernando Valley in Southern California, in addition to his rounds as a farrier.

If you want to combine book knowledge and practical skills, there are some things to look for when choosing a school: how many students per teacher in each class, the number of horses actually trimmed or shod during the course, cost, length of course, how much time spent in forge work compared to time spent shoeing or trimming, depth of theory taught—anatomy and physiology, history, disease, injury, nutrition, restraint, horseowner relationships, horse psychology, business management—and general reputation of the school.

If you choose a school with care, you'll give yourself a firm foundation on which to build your skills. Correspondence courses or a three to five day "short course" or clinics are also available to supplement your work, but can't take the place of long-term experience and study.

What Can You Earn and What Are the Working Hours?

Because farriers are usually self-employed, it takes time to accumulate customers. People are often reluctant to change farriers or to accept someone new into the field. But this is sometimes just a matter of time. If your work is good and if you're persistent and friendly, you'll make it. At first you may work long hours and not earn much, but once you're established you can choose the hours you want to work and how much you'll charge. Rates vary from as little as $5 for just trimming without shoeing, to $26 for normal, straightforward shoeing, and as much as $75 for gaited horses, where shoes are individually hand made. An average farrier can shoe from six to ten horses a day. Some may do more. This depends on the driving distance between jobs, the quality of the work, and the temperament of the horses.

Where Can You Expect to Work?

Some farriers have a central blacksmith shop where the horses are brought for shoeing. More often, however, farriers turn a pickup truck or van into a blacksmith shop on wheels. This al-

Durie displays her tools on the back of her pickup.

lows them to move from one location to another with ease. Boarding stables, breeding farms, training stables, racetracks, farms, ranches, and backyards are among their many stops. A few work for a salary or fixed fee paid by a farm or stable. Others work at a racetrack and confine their practice to that one location. There are no rules. The work day depends on what the individual wants to do and what jobs are available.

What Can You Do Now to Prepare for a Career as a Farrier?

"Work with animals in any way you can," suggests Pete Beckman. "The more you are around horses and all phases of the business—training, riding, sale barns—the more experience you'll get. It's one of those things that just gets in your blood. You can't get away from it.

"If you're fortunate enough to own a horse, get to know all about it, including feeding habits, care, and maintenance. Go to shows, observe, watch the judges react, and pay attention to the various horses."

You'll also need experience handling the tools of the trade. Become familiar with files, hammers, chisels, and punches. High school or vocational school courses in hot metal working or blacksmithing are also valuable. Physical science, particularly anatomy, some public relations exposure, and basic business management are also helpful to your overall success.

What Is the Future of Farriery?

"The trade has never been better," claims Pete Beckman. "We have more horses in the United States than ever before." Since most horses require trimming or shoeing every six to eight weeks, the demand is great for dedicated and competent farriers.

Although there is plenty of work, farriery is not a get-rich-quick profession and it is not easy. It involves heavy physical labor, constant danger, and it requires a high level of skill, as well as an ability to think, reason, and recall information quickly.

The rewards, however, are great. Farriery offers plenty of opportunity and flexibility. As a result, successful professionals are able to choose where they want to work, what to specialize in, and how much time they want to devote to their career.

If you'd like more information about this expanding profession, and a list of farrier schools in the United States, write to:

>American Farrier's Association
>P.O. Box 695
>Albuquerque, New Mexico 87103

3

Racetrack Careers

The California Horse Racing Institute in Newhall, California, is the only school of its kind in the United States. Students from nine to thirty-five learn from books, by observation, and by practice how to become a jockey.

Jim and Rita Fresquez, the youthful husband and wife team that owns the jockey school, have been around horses all their lives. Jim, a state-licensed horse trainer and jockey instructor, has trained racehorses for about ten years. Rita began riding when she was five and was involved in horse shows, rode polo ponies, and has galloped the racetrack exercising horses. Jim was in Northern California the day I interviewed Rita, but she shared some of his views and his expertise about the business.

Working at the jockey school is a third partner, Susan Liebow, a petite brunette, who is an expert trainer and horsewoman. Glenda Cormie is another employee now working toward her trainer's license. She is currently a riding instructor.

The school came about out of Jim's and Rita's experience with horses. At one time, a movie studio contacted Jim about

Rita Fresquez, owner of The California Horse Racing Institute in Newhall, California.

training two stunt girls for a Black Beauty movie. While on this project, the idea of a jockey school occurred to them. They wanted to organize a place where they could teach young people to ride racehorses.

They ran an ad for the school at first. The initial response was overwhelming. "We were bombarded with applications," said Rita, smiling, and still a bit awed at their rapid growth. "From there we sat down, planned a curriculum, and organized classes and practice sessions on the track."

The school is unique because of the extensive formal education in riding, care and grooming of horses, and even some classes in the anatomy and physiology of the horse.

The basic course takes six weeks and costs $250. Students come to the sessions four times a week, three evenings and one full day, where they learn grooming, mounting, dismounting, walking, and galloping a horse. This course is followed by the advanced training which costs $175 a month, and specializes in treating each student individually. During this portion of the program, students are ready to go onto the oval half-mile track equipped with railings and a starting gate. There they learn the fine points of track riding, concentration, and the art of breaking from the gate. The school's purpose is to prepare students carefully and methodically in every facet of the training necessary to become a jockey.

"The first thing we do is give them a basic lecture on horsemanship," explained Rita. "We interview the students first to see if they've had any experience with horses. Ninety percent of our students have never even touched a horse before. Two of

Horse training trio. Left to right: Glenda Cormie, riding instructor; Susan Liebow, co-owner and trainer; and Rita Fresquez, owner.

our boys who are now jockeys had never ridden a horse before they came to us last year. They couldn't even lead a horse with the halter. So the first thing we do is teach them how to halter a horse, how to pick his hooves, and how to groom. We teach them about legs, and we go over the entire conformation of a horse and all the physiology, bridling, and grooming, before they're ready to get on the horse. We don't put anyone up until they know exactly how to work around the animal. When the rider is secure, the horse will be too."

Physical Characteristics and Qualifications

The important physical characteristics of a jockey include a short, small frame, good conditioning, and a fit body. According to Rita, being a jockey "does not require so much physical strength as it does *fitness*."

Discipline and drive are perhaps even more important. Without them you won't make it as a professional.

After the schooling is completed, the first thing a student must do is get a license for riding at a racetrack prior to qualifying as a professional jockey. The best preparation for this is to ride as many horses a day as you can so you will know every kind of horse there is. By the time you actually get the license, you'll have had a great deal of experience—perhaps six to eight months or more, riding twelve to fourteen horses a day.

Most people take three to four years to qualify as a jockey, but two of Rita's students got their apprentice licenses within one year from the time they completed the course. These were unusual cases, however.

One of their prize students, Ellie Shrimp, is a real phenomenon at the age of sixteen. She came to the school when she was fifteen and worked hard. She stayed with Rita all summer, went to the track every morning at 6:00 to exercise the horses, went to Del Mar Race Track and then to the Pomona Fair. Following that expedition, she joined Jim at their place in Northern California where she exercised horses daily. From there she moved on to Hollywood Park as an exerciser. Today Ellie can handle anything. "She's on her way," said Rita with pride. "She's really on her way."

The Business Side

Horse racing is big business. Between 75 percent and 80 percent of California's revenue comes from horse racing. Billions of dollars are spent at betting every year.

A jockey is usually paid a percentage of the purse. If he comes in first, he gets 10 percent of the purse. Second place merits $55 and third brings $45. From that place down jockeys receive $35. However, if a jockey wins a big race he will naturally get a big bonus. And that's where a jockey can make a lot of money.

Horse racing is a very intricate business. If you move on a racehorse when he's working flat out you can break his leg. "You have to be that still," Rita told us. "One of the reasons officials and trainers like our school," she added, "is our thoroughness. We send them kids who know how to take care of a horse. They know the feel and they're able to tell the trainer how the horse responds."

Although a jockey does not have much to do with the care of a horse, he does need to know a great deal about the physiology and anatomy of the animal.

"The important parts of the racehorse are the two front legs," Rita said. "If you don't know those legs, you can't tell if he's going sore or where he's breaking down. All this the jockey has to learn, and the only way to learn is from the physiology of

Student runs horse as part of his schooling to become a jockey.

the horse. Every professional jockey can tell if a horse is shin-bucking, if he's breaking down in the ankle, or if he's sore in the knee or tendon. It's just a feel you get when you're galloping —a sixth sense. I can ride a racehorse on the track and tell when that horse is just not right, even if I don't feel any heat or swelling in the leg, ankle, or knee. You really become one with the horse," said Rita.

If a student doesn't know what he or she is doing, nobody is going to put him or her on a horse worth $150,000. The jockey school is the best form of preparation for this career because when students complete the course of study they know what they are doing. They get their licenses, practice on less expensive

37

Susan Liebow, petite trainer at California Horse Racing Institute where all aspects of equine care and racing are taught.

horses, and then, "When they get that experience," says Rita, "their hands become gold!"

Not only do the Fresquezes teach students how to become jockeys, they also prepare them for other track-related jobs such as groom and exerciser. A little jockey, for example, is not physically able to gallop large, tough horses. It would ruin their racing. Therefore, exercisers fill a real need. Since horse racing is such a big money industry, it's absolutely essential to have qualified expert horsemen and women at all levels.

Trainer

In horse training, brains count more than muscle, even though it is a very physically demanding job. Endless patience, courage, and a good working knowledge of horses is also important. Basic training techniques apply to all horses whether they perform at the racetrack, in shows and rodeos, or are ridden strictly for pleasure.

Training involves learning to understand the horse as an individual, since riding each horse is a new experience. A trainer must know what to do, how much of it to do, and then be able to tell if the horse understood what you wanted him to do. This is called getting the "feel of the horse." This quality is probably the most difficult and the most desired in training and riding. It comes with practice and confidence and takes many hours in the saddle on many different horses to acquire it.

Four points of contact are important parts of training a horse. They are the trainer's two hands and two feet. These points directly influence the movements of the horse. The hands influence the horse's head, neck, and mouth. And the legs and heels will directly influence the horse's body. For the greatest control, the trainer must learn to balance hand and foot cues to complement each other.

When working with a colt, it is a major undertaking for a trainer just to get a halter on the weanling that is not long off the dam. At first the trainer attaches a soft "catch-rope" about six feet long to the halter. It's important at this point to talk to the horse softly, move him around in the stall, and walk around him slowly. This process takes about a week. Next, the trainer gradually introduces the colt to the barn, as he or she leads the horse up and down the shavings-covered floor. To teach a young horse to stand tied, a trainer will sometimes begin by tieing the horse to a rubber innertube.

After several months, usually eight, the young horse is turned into the breaking pen and worked loose. After it is used to being restrained, the trainer introduces the snaffle bit and the longe line for short periods at a time.

The colt's daily routine is usually no more than thirty minutes. This includes being led from the barn, stopped, squared up, trotted beside his handler, brought to a brisk halt, set up, trotted again, and worked loose or on the hand line. Repetition is important so that later when the horse is ready for shows, there is a consistent pattern of movement.

Success as a trainer comes with experience and know-how. Formal education is important for horsemen, but the ability to train and handle horses cannot be learned from books.

You can get a salaried job training for one individual, or ranch, or you can work as a public trainer. Working on a salary means a regular paycheck and fewer expenses. Working as a public trainer, however, means you are your own boss, you can do as you please, and you can often earn more money than when you work for someone else. But your expenses are usually greater and you must provide your own arena, place to live, trailers, trucks, and other supplies.

Exerciser

Exercisers play an important part in the racing business. Their preparation is the same as that of a jockey. In fact, many of the students at a jockey school become exercisers because they are not qualified in size or weight to be professional jockeys.

The exerciser's basic duties include riding the horses, sometimes as many as ten to twelve a day, early in the morning, usually before 8:00. Basically, they give the horses a complete workout on the track, working with commands in the same way a jockey does.

Some of the Fresquezes' students, such as sixteen-year-old Ellie

Shrimp, for example, become exercise riders after completing their training at the jockey school. The excellent preparation they get on the track and in the classroom gives them a definite advantage over less-trained individuals. It can take as much as three to four years to get a job as an exerciser if a young person does not display the necessary skills when he or she applies for work at a track. Students who can start from a gate and show promise for a future as a jockey can move into the field quickly. This is usually the result of formal training such as the Fresquezes provide at their school. If a young person has no training and no contacts at a track, about the only way to get started is to go directly to the track and apply for work. First jobs are usually menial and include walking hot horses and/or cleaning stalls.

Racetrack Groom

A groom is basically a caretaker. To a groom the welfare of the horse is his or her main concern. And from the ranks of grooms and trainers come some leading professionals. Therefore, anyone studying to become a jockey will learn to groom a horse at the start.

Professional grooms are with their horses nearly twenty-four hours a day. Because of this constant watch and care a groom needs understanding, patience, and love of horses.

One of the duties of a groom is to go over the horse carefully every day to make sure that no boots, which are rubber protection for a horse's legs used to avoid injury or chafing during running or jumping, have begun chafing, no nails have pricked the soles of the feet, and that the horse is eating and eliminating properly. The groom and the trainer work together. It is up to the groom to report any abnormal findings to the trainer. Some situations may need medical attention, others may be minor.

The trainer will make the final decision. The groom simply lets the trainer know the condition of the horse.

Grooms are also responsible for keeping the stalls clean. Bedding, usually made of straw or good-quality sawdust, must be deep enough to be comfortable, providing a good cushion when the horse lies down, and yet not so deep that it is awkward for the horse to move around in it.

After the horse has been fed and watered and the stall cleaned (or mucked) out, the day's work begins. Before the horse is walked, jogged, trained, or raced the first step is the same. He must be cleaned up. This consists of cleaning out the feet, brushing the body, and straightening the mane and tail. After brushing, a groom will usually go over the entire body with a rub cloth to remove any loose dirt.

In cleaning the horse's body, three tools are used: two brushes

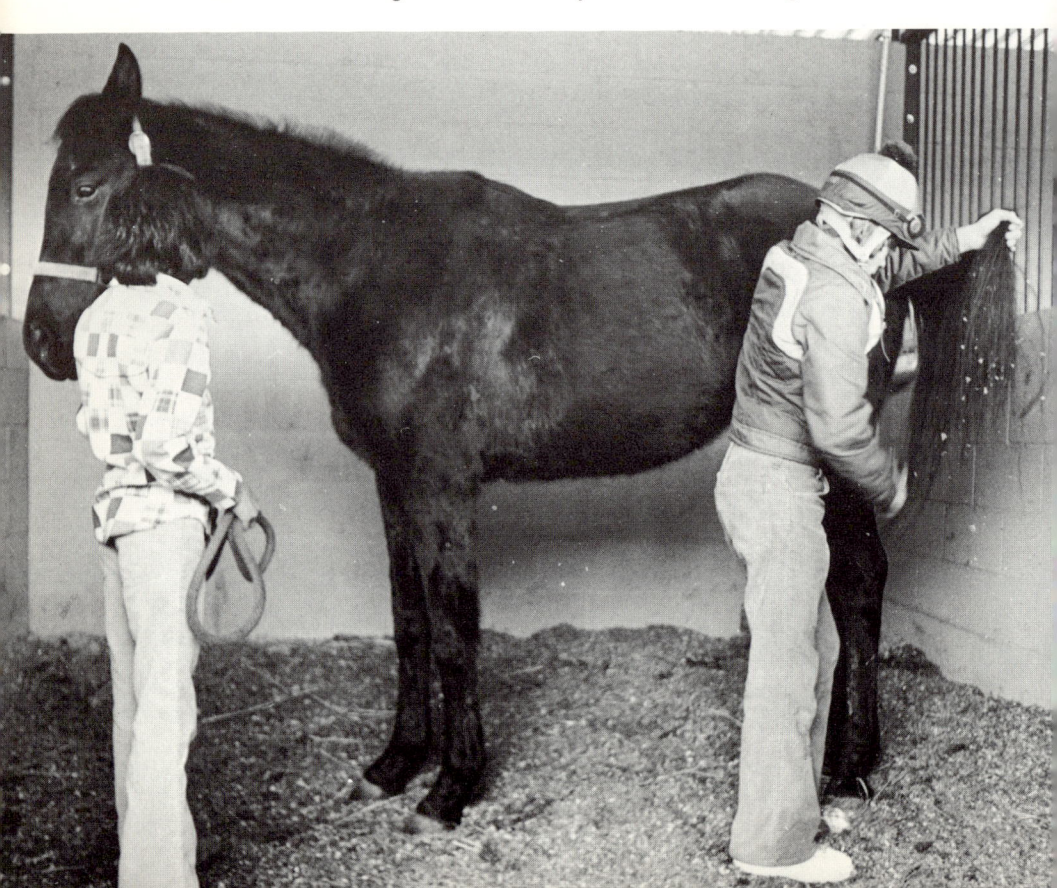

Students learn to groom horses as part of their training.

and a currycomb. A soft-bristled brush is used for the body; a stiff-bristled brush for the mane and tail; and a currycomb, either metal or rubber, which fits a groom's hand, for loosening the skin and stirring the hair just before brushing.

Preparing a horse for his daily events, cooling him down, bathing him, and looking after his equipment are other chores which require many hours. At times the job may seem tedious and tiring, but after a groom learns his tasks the routine is not as heavy as it looks at first.

"A good groom means a great deal to any racing stable," says author and groom, Sanders Russell, in a recent article. "No phase of racing is more important than learning how to take care of a horse properly so he remains sound, healthy, and happy throughout the training and racing season."

Harness Racing

Harness racing is another fast-growing track sport. It has doubled its attendance in the last ten years and the figures continue to mount. At one time harness racing was nothing more than a pleasant family outing at a county or state fair. Today, however, it is a big league sport and business operating in major cities throughout the country.

Harness racing differs from thoroughbred racing, although in both sports the object is the same—to win the race. Thoroughbreds run or gallop. Harness horses must maintain a specified gait and they are guided by a driver seated in a jog cart or racing bike sometimes called a sulky. The "gait" refers to trotting or pacing, specific methods of movement that are peculiar to the Standardbred or harness horse. Maintaining high speeds at a specified gait takes long months of intensive training.

To qualify as a harness racing driver you would most likely

begin as a groom. Many top drivers started their careers this way. A summer job at a track would provide excellent experience and give you an opportunity to learn about the profession from licensed drivers and trainers.

As in all other areas of the horse industry, it is necessary to begin by learning to care for the horse. Proper training, feeding, shoeing, equipment, and handling are important aspects that every driver must know. Each horse is different. Some are quiet and easy to handle, others jumpy and nervous. Only experience provides a student with the "feel" he or she needs to see what harness racing is all about. You must be sixteen to work at a track and probably the best approach is to simply contact the nearest harness track and talk to the trainers and drivers there about getting started.

For more information you can also write to:

> The United States Trotting Association
> 750 Michigan Avenue
> Columbus, Ohio 43215

They publish a very helpful booklet titled "Your Key to Harness Racing," which is free for the asking. Your questions will be answered and the Association will also include the requirements for becoming a licensed harness driver.

The Future of the Horse Racing Business

The racetrack business is definitely open to anyone who is willing to learn the business and to acquire the necessary skills. There are opportunities for new jockeys, drivers, grooms, and exercisers. However, it is a very competitive field.

"The real money in the horse industry is in racing," says Rita Fresquez. "But it has to be approached correctly. It has to be done so the horse is not injured. In order to avoid injury you have to put out horsemen and women who know the animals and who truly care for them."

For more information about the California Horse Racing Institute, contact Rita and Jim Fresquez at the address below:

>California Horse Racing Institute
>P.O. Box 417
>Newhall, California 91321

You may wish to write to the Jockey's Guild for further material on the profession:

>National Managing Director
>Jockey's Guild, Inc.
>555 Fifth Avenue
>New York, New York 10017

And if you are interested in pursuing information about racetrack management, contact the University of Arizona. They have an excellent and thorough program of instruction in all phases of horse care and racetrack management. Write to:

>University of Arizona
>College of Agriculture—Bldg. No. 36
>Tucson, Arizona 85721

Horse shows are popular weekend activities during Southern California's warm winters. Here a hunter finishes the course as two competitors look on.

4

Horse Show Occupations

A beautiful Sunday afternoon may draw a hundred or more people to a horse show. Sleek and well-groomed animals pace nervously, riders adjust their caps and straighten their hunt coats before the event begins. Entries have been processed, grounds readied, jumping courses laid out. It looks effortless to the outsider. But only the judge, ringmaster, announcer, publicity committee, and show manager know what makes it work—team effort.

The trophy committee, for example, has to come up with awards that are within the club's budget and that please the participants. Entries have to be taken, publicity sent out, and an announcer hired—someone with a clear voice, stage presence, and the ability to read correctly the names of the entrants.

If you're interested in participating in horse shows as a young person, you may find a career behind the scenes something you'd like to pursue as an adult.

Show Officials

Officers of a Recognized Show generally include a president, vice president, secretary, and treasurer. The show administration also has an executive committee, special committees, a show secretary, and a show manager. The officials include the officers, judges, stewards, and timekeepers.

Other show personnel include a ringmaster, recorder, announcer, blacksmith, "in" and "out" gatemen, jump crew, manager, and veterinarian.

In a Recognized Show it is necessary to appoint one or more AHSA (American Horse Shows Association) stewards. They are representatives of the AHSA and approved by the stewards' committee of that organization. Only recognized stewards in good standing may officiate at Recognized Shows.

Their duties include:
- —Verifying the enforcement of Association rules.
- —Protecting the interests of exhibitors.
- —Reporting to the directors of the show any offense or violation of the rules.
- —Writing a report regarding the show within three days after it has been completed.

Their responsibilities include:
- —Verifying that all jumper courses conform to the minimum requirements.
- —Verifying the weighing of riders in classes that require minimum weights.
- —Supervising and recording "time-out" for problems that might occur, such as a horse casting a shoe or the breaking of equipment.
- —Requesting that the judge seek veterinary advice if it seems necessary.

Judges' stand at a horse show.

Next, a good show must have a judge, someone who can evaluate pace, manners, and jumping ability. A person who is capable of making a living as a trainer, exhibitor, or breeder will usually make a fine judge.

Every horse show should have the best judge money can buy. And there is a real demand for qualified individuals who take their responsibilities seriously and keep themselves up-to-date on trends among the various breeds. The pay is good too. Recommended minimum pay for an approved judge is expenses plus $100 a day for nine hours or less, and $10 an hour for each hour over nine.

Judges have a variety of duties during a horse show. They have the authority to place horses in whatever position in a class they think suitable. And each judge is responsible for tallying the entries, scores, etc., and reporting these figures to the American Horse Shows Association (AHSA) if it is an officially sponsored show. A judge may also order any person or horse from the competition for bad conduct.

There are often complaints about judges in one form or another at local and state or national competitions. Many participants feel that the qualifications for judges are not strictly enforced and that many mean well but don't really know what they are doing. If this is true, it's apparent that there are good opportunities for knowledgeable people who want to become horse show judges. Show committees will always be in search of a qualified person who understands and exhibits sound horsemanship, knows the various breeds, and enjoys working with riders as well.

Recognized judges are grouped in three classifications: registered (senior), recorded (junior), and guest. In each case the judge must be over twenty-one years of age. Anyone with a sound background in equitation can apply to the American Horse Shows Association for recognition as a judge. Licensing requires a written test and references from several registered judges. Acceptance is based on experience, ability, judgment, and character. The judges' committee of the AHSA then classifies the applicant as a registered or recorded judge—or refuses acceptance.

A guest judge is an individual member of the AHSA not enrolled as a judge. He or she receives special permission from the AHSA to officiate as a registered judge at a particular show for that show only.

Competitor in motion before the judges.

Helen Kitner Crabtree, a national saddle horse authority, commented in a recent magazine interview on what she thought contributed to the greatest possible fairness in horse show judging: "Hire qualified judges who have the courage of their own experience and judgment." And she added, "It is the show's obligation to provide ring conditions conducive to good performances."

After the judge, a good ringmaster or ring steward is next in importance. They have the task of seeing that the show runs smoothly and efficiently. In many respects, being a ringmaster is a thankless job, and not usually one that requires a full-time commitment. Ringmasters cover almost as much ground at a horse show as the horses! They must see to every detail and are a kind of go-between for the announcer and judge.

Ringmasters get the classes ready for the judge, making sure they present themselves on time and in order. They provide the judges with all the necessary information so they can pick the winners without difficulty. This includes names, numbers, and so on. The ringmaster focuses on the judge during the entire show and does whatever is necessary to make the judge's job as effortless as possible. He or she also delivers the judge's messages to the announcer and must be fully responsible for all of the activity in the arena, controlling the conduct of the horses and the exhibitors.

It is a rewarding job in many ways because a horse show cannot run efficiently without a good ringmaster who has a sense of humor as well as responsibility, a love of horses, and a fondness for people.

The show manager can be any reputable person who can furnish proof that he or she is capable through ability and experience. This job involves enforcing all rules referring to the show or contest. Managers are in charge of mailing all entry blanks, premium lists, and catalogs, and enforcing the arrival and departure times of the show participants.

Making sure the horses, exhibitors, officials, and spectators are comfortable is another task for the show manager. And he or she is responsible for maintaining clean and orderly conditions throughout the show or contest.

When the show is completed, the manager gets a marked copy of the judging program signed by both the judge (or judges) and the ringmaster, and it is kept for at least two years.

There are approximately four hundred horse shows recognized by the American Horse Shows Association which is the governing body of horse shows. Nearly every young person who rides dreams of being involved in one of them someday. Many of the horse shows on any given weekend during the summer are sponsored by local horsemen's associations, charitable organizations, and saddle clubs. To have a successful event takes the combined efforts of a good many people.

If working in horse shows interests you, contact the AHSA for more information on the particular job you'd like to pursue.

>The American Horse Shows Association
>527 Madison Avenue
>New York, New York 10022

5

Training Riding Horses and Teaching Young People to Ride

Riding instructor Corrine MacDougall has been involved with horses most of her life. She learned to ride at the age of six, and at seventeen entered statewide competition and became California State Champion in English and All-around, and Reserve Champion in the Western division.

At the present time she teaches riding at her home in the hills of Calabasas, California, where she lives with her husband and children. "The best way to get into this business," says Corrine, "is to start at any stable where you can get basic horsemanship—not just riding. This includes anatomy, proper grooming, naming tack and equipment, and handling of a horse. To become a good horseman, not just a good rider, you need to expose yourself as often and as much as possible to horses in general. Tag along with a vet. Hang around a stable."

With a good general background in equitation you can move into almost any phase of the horse business. To become an instructor you need a thorough grounding in riding itself. "Basic equitation or horsemanship is the same whether you ride West-

Riding instructor and stable owner, Corrine MacDougall.

ern, English, or Saddleseat," said Corrine. There are some differences but the basics are the same.

One thing she emphasizes is that to become a competent horseman takes time. "It's not something you can learn overnight. You have to care about horses, like what you're doing, and be willing to learn slowly. There are a lot of good schools where you can get a degree in horsemanship, but all the book learning is no substitute for the actual work. I would say it takes about ten years to be a complete horseman. Ten years of experience—and experience is the only way you can get real knowledge."

Preparing the Horse

Corrine trains some of the horses she uses for riding instruc-

Corrine works horse in arena where she trains and gives lessons.

tion. The first step in handling a baby horse, or foal, is to get it used to people. Leading a foal with a halter encourages it to follow rather than tug at the rope. "The more you handle them at this early age the better," says Corrine. "There are no ninety-day wonders in training horses. You have to break them in easy. For example, at first you get them used to a blanket, then a saddle, and next acquaint them with a bit by just putting it in the mouth and letting the horse hold it for awhile." Another device she uses is called the longe line. This is a long line used to walk, trot, or lope the horse around you in a circle.

Corrine feels strongly about not letting a horse buck, rear, or do anything that is induced by fear. "If a horse is afraid of you, he'll do anything to protect himself."

During the first and second year Corrine gets the horse used to tack and equipment, and also ground drives him. This involves putting a snaffle bit in his mouth, then standing on the ground behind the horse urging it along with two long reins. This teaches the horse to move forward and to back up. Only after these methods does Corrine allow anyone in the saddle.

"I feel it's best to wait until after the second year to put someone on the horse's back," says Corrine. "I usually allow one of my experienced riders to get on first while I hold the horse below. That way there is no chance for bucking."

Training as a profession does not pay well at first, according to Corrine. However, opportunity is available and good trainers will always be in demand. The best way to get into the field is to approach a training stable or school and offer some service in exchange for learning the trade. You could shovel manure, groom, clean stalls, or do whatever odd jobs come up. "A lot of young people feel that being in the saddle is the most important part of it. But it's just as necessary to establish ground work with a horse before you get on its back," says Corrine.

Riding Instruction in Her Own Backyard

Currently, Corrine spends several afternoons a week teaching groups of children and a few adults to ride. "I get my students by word of mouth," she says. "I've never advertised. I know some of the big schools do, but I don't because I hadn't really planned on teaching as a profession. I just happen to love children and horses, and the two go together."

Corrine fell into instructing almost accidentally. People began noticing her schooling and training her own horses and children several years ago. Gradually, they began asking her to teach their children to ride. Since she had been in the horse show profession for a long time, instructing came naturally.

According to Corrine, beginners are the most difficult group to work with. "You're dealing with live creatures. The horse has a mind of its own and so does the child. It's very important to fit the two personalities together."

Some students take longer than others to feel at ease with horses, but no matter what their ability, all of them can have fun with the sport. "Enjoyment is the main thing to get out of horsemanship," according to Corrine. Then she added, "I also find that being around horses and handling them gives children a sense of accomplishment, security, and self-expression that they just can't get anywhere else. I've had little kids that were shy and withdrawn get on a horse, and as they learn to ride and master the animal, their personalities developed and changed. It's marvelous to watch."

Teaching riding in your backyard is one way to have a career as an instructor, but there are other ways too. You can work for

Horse out for a romp and training session.

a dude ranch and give lessons to guests, teach riding at local stables, where students come to you and use the horses provided by the stable owners, or work for a boarding stable and give instruction to riders who board their horses at that location.

    There are also openings in animal science departments at state universities, group instruction for equestrian classes at the high school and college level, and special techniques for those interested in learning trick riding, barrel racing, rodeo riding, circus acts, and so on. Getting into these specialized fields of instruction, however, usually requires your own expertise in a particular area. And this comes with practice, exposure, and a willingness to work your way up through the ranks. Again, opportunities present themselves to individuals who spend time around horses, ride frequently, answer advertisements for instructors, and to those willing to follow leads and suggestions from others in the field. Sometimes you can get started by working for another instructor and taking the overflow of students until your own business builds up.

6

Training Circus Horses

"If you have *got* to be an animal trainer," says Wally Ross, trainer for Circus Vargas, "be one and be a good one. But if you just want to train animals, forget it—this work is usually more heartbreaking than rewarding."

The rewards for Wally, however, are obvious. He is an expert at what he does, a man who loves his work. After talking with me at his compound in Thousand Oaks, California, Wally showed us an act incorporating six horses that had been "absolutely wild and never touched by human hands" before Wally got them.

"This is one profession that should belong to the young people," said Wally, "but it actually belongs to the middle-aged and past. I never accomplished much until I was in my late thirties and early forties. I'm fifty-one now. There's not much money in it—for years and years. You can go hungry training animals. When you start getting older the jobs are more available and the pay is better, but then you lose most of your get-up-and-go. That's why I feel it's a profession for the young, people from their late teens through their twenties."

Wally got his start training animals during World War II. "I didn't make it in the service, so that left me at home. Jobs were fantastically easy to get then. And many people said that I had a gift from God to handle animals. I never had to learn a lot of the things other people do. I seemed to already know how."

At the age of seventeen Wally left home with a circus—Buck Owen's Wild West Show and Circus. His father didn't approve, so he sent the State Patrol after him. They brought Wally back but the next day he left again. When his dad tracked Wally down this time, the boss horse trainer told his dad that if he allowed Wally to stay he'd see to it that he worked his tail off, and he'd make sure Wally wrote a penny postcard home every Sunday. Wally did just that: he learned how to train horses and from there he went on to other jobs. Things began to fall into place for him. He trained the first porpoise to be of assistance to man in the ocean, and he turned loose the first sea lion for a practical test in the ocean. "Some of my training techniques and props are no longer used," said Wally, remembering, "but I did establish some firsts that I'm very proud of."

Training a Wild Horse

"I've always wanted to train wild horses," said Wally, showing us the six in his current circus act. The first thing Wally does with an absolutely wild horse is halter and tie him up. "They must first learn to stand tied up willingly. Then you get your hands on them and gentle both sides."

Wally trained the group in a record five months. And then they were turned out to pasture. "I train each one individually, then two at a time, and so on. I worked eight and ten hours a day on all six. I work one while five rest. And believe me," said

Left: *Circus trainer, Wally Ross, in barn after a rain.*

Below: *Wally works horses for a liberty act.*

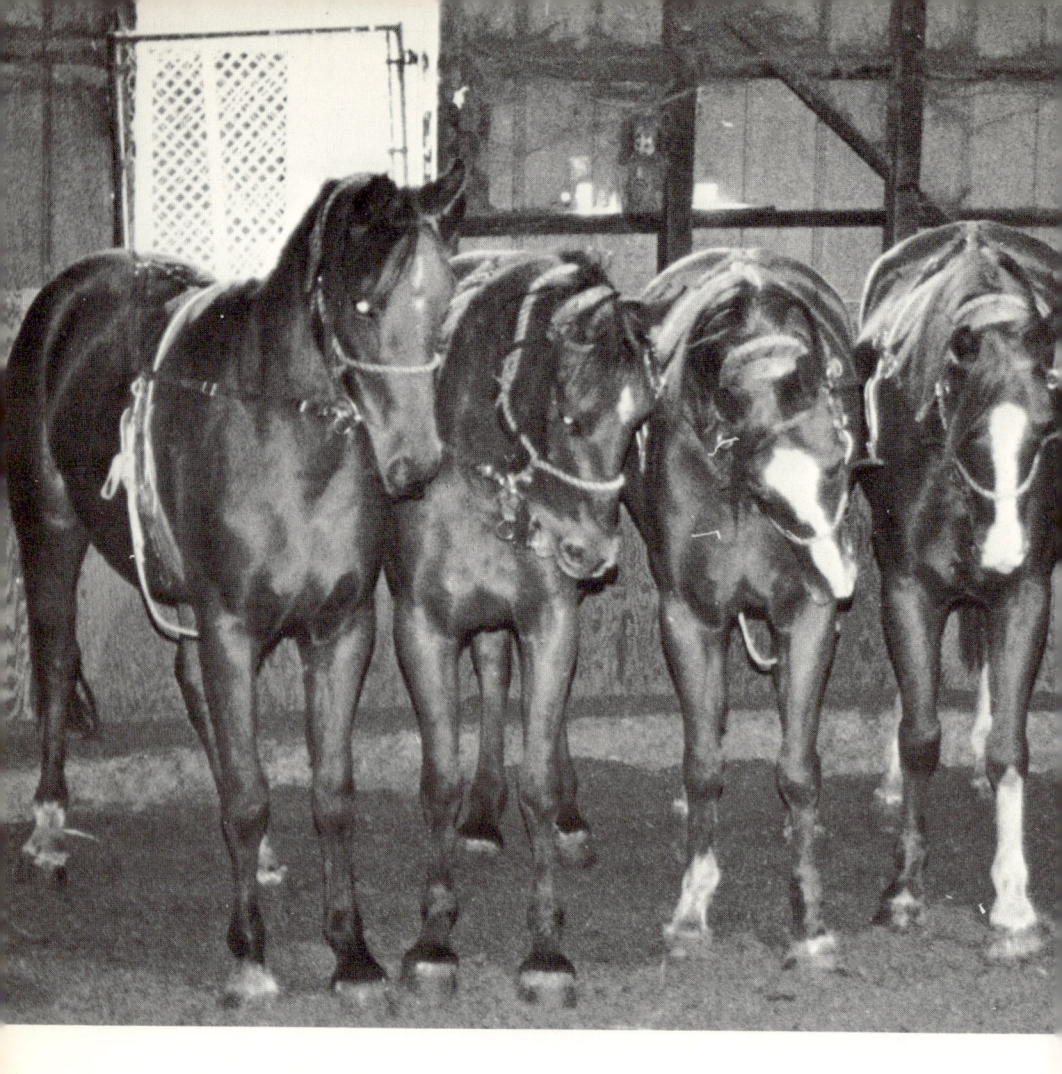

Wally with a deep breath, "six horses can outwork me. They're still going and I'm exhausted!"

The horses do not learn from one another. They each learn their routine one at a time. "And then you put them in a ring two at a time and they forget everything. Then three at a time and then six at a time."

Wally uses body movement and words to signal the horses. "Someday you might be working with a twenty-piece brass band

Wally Ross's summer project—training six Arabians for a liberty act.

right behind you, so words have to be insignificant. You must have a body movement cue that the horses recognize and respond to."

The techniques Wally uses have been going on since the days of the Roman Empire. "Performing on horseback is as old as recorded history." Circular acts with performing horses, ring curb, and other exhibitions go back to the Circus Maximus and the Roman Games.

65

Breaking into the Field

"I think all young people should start from the ground up," said Wally firmly. "You need to learn stable techniques and the care and handling of a horse before you can ever consider being a trainer." It's something that has to come from your gut level. "I'll break my arm patting myself on the back," said Wally with a big grin, "but I believe that animal training is an art and only gifted people will stick to it long enough to be successful."

In addition to training horses, Wally also teaches exotic animal training at Moorpark College in Moorpark, California. Unlike others, he does not believe in any classroom work. "When students train with me," said Wally, "it's all lab work, all outdoor field experience. In fact, we even work in the ring. All outdoors."

Only second-year students work with Wally. Before they reach his lab they've studied care and handling, diet, and basic veterinary care or preventive medicine. Then they are ready to learn training techniques. "I don't teach any animal trainers," added Wally, "I just teach people to *become* animal trainers. They have to do that for themselves. After they leave my class, they're capable of training animals. Then it's up to them."

Jobs at the present time are scarce. Perhaps the only approach is to make copies of your resume and start mailing them to every available animal-related industry. Wally suggests contacting circuses, rodeos, amusement parks, zoos—every possible place that has animals. Some will answer.

The prospects for work as a trainer are poor according to Wally Ross, but like any other profession those who want it badly enough will stay with it until they find work. "The people who really want to be animal trainers will make it," said Wally. "*Really* want to be," he stressed. "Those who just wish they could, will not."

Dorothy Herbert, well-known female trainer, now retired.

Lady Equestrian

Dorothy Herbert is one of the world's foremost female equestrians. She is retired now and talked about her days in the training arena.

"I got into this business when I was fourteen years old," said Dorothy. "I was born in Louisville, Kentucky. My family raised and trained horses. One day I was riding in a horse show and a talent scout for Ringling Brothers Circus was there. He asked me to try out for the circus. I went along, made it, and I've been in the circus business ever since."

Dorothy doesn't feel that approach would work today. "The only way you can make it now is to find somebody that's interested in young people. For example, at one point I worked in San Francisco at the zoo. We had a program there where we did train young folks. We put on a show and called it a Zoocus. We had a bareback act, horses, trained dogs, ponies, birds, and aerial acts. We used all college kids then. And when younger children wanted to participate, we'd let them handle some of the equipment and begin training animals themselves under supervision."

Reflecting on the good old days in the circus, Dorothy talked about how things worked. "We used to travel by train," she said. "You could go to bed at night and when you'd get up you'd be in the next town. But not anymore. Now everything's done by truck. There's just too much driving. It's pretty hard to drive all night and still have enthusiasm for the show the next day."

Although Dorothy agrees with Wally that there isn't much work available in the circus world, she does feel that there is still ample opportunity to make money training jumping horses. "Jumping was my specialty," she added, "and there is a big market for that at the moment."

In no area of riding is willingness on the part of the horse as important as it is in jumping. Nothing is more satisfying to watch (or ride) than a horse whose approach is calm, relaxed, confident and certain, responsive and reliable.

Getting a horse to this point depends on the trainer. And today there is a big market for training jumping horses, teaching students to ride and jump in shows. Sound training skills and the ability to know the difference between correction and punishment are important qualities for any good trainer. You begin by laying a basic foundation in unmounted schooling of the horse, then build slowly and patiently to mounted work.

Time, patience, mental and emotional stability, as well as physical ability are necessary. Training a horse to jump is challenging. And not all horses have the potential to become good jumpers. Veterinary routine, the blacksmith program, and basic stable management all play a part in judging a horse's potential.

The main goal in training jumpers is to get them to be willing to jump. This willingness eliminates many of the hazards that are often associated with jumping. When a horse accepts jumping as a part of his regular routine, it puts this aspect of his performance into perspective. It becomes just one more phase of the overall riding program and not something to be approached with fear or nervousness.

There are many young people who want to compete in Jumping Class, who need special instruction in this area, who are anxious to work their horses toward this goal. You could supply this service.

If you view training as teaching, not punishing, if you enjoy the problems, opportunities, and challenges of schooling jumpers, then this could be a very satisfying specialty.

Young Trainer at Work

Tina Risdon, a recent graduate of Moorpark's exotic animal program, works with Wally Ross now and Circus Vargas. She is specializing in horses at this time. "I've always been interested in animals," said Tina. "I'd been around them all my life. I wanted something different, more exciting than domestic animals, so I enrolled in the college program but didn't make it until one year later. You have to go through a personal interview to find out if you're dedicated enough to do all the things necessary."

The first year involves a lot of physical labor. And it includes the basics—feeding and cleaning the animals and so on. "You don't get to actually handle any animals until late in the second semester." Tina had been a Western rider and English was all

Tina Risdon in costume. She rides dressage and works the liberty act for Circus Vargas.

new to her, so she had some things to learn as she moved into horse training. Specific training techniques are part of the second year in the program. At the end of the first year of study students take over the animals that the second year students have trained and simply maintain those behaviors. "You're not really training," said Tina, "you're just maintaining.

"There is a lot of book work the first year. And the first animal you train is a rat," added Tina. From there she graduated in size to horses. "I started working for the circus in June of 1977 and started training my first horse in September. But that was just in my spare time." In between Tina cleaned, fed, or did whatever came up. Her actual training time amounted to only about one hour a day.

"I probably work now about two hours a day. And the horse's training is all from his back. I worked strictly from the ground at first, getting all the behaviors down before the saddle work. It's easier that way," said Tina.

Tina remarked on the large number of tools that are available to trainers. The whip, ropes, a broom, broomhandle are just a few.

I noticed Tina using a variety of hand movements with the horses. She combines her movements with certain pieces of equipment. "The crop and such are incorporated into the behavior so that the horse knows that he's supposed to behave in a certain way. Vocal commands also play an important part but are never substituted for the trainer's body movement. That's what counts most," added Tina.

Although jobs are scarce, Tina Risdon is one example of a young person who knew what she wanted and went after the job. If you're interested in this kind of work, you might begin contacting every place you can think of that could give you a lead on getting started in the animal training field. It's also a good idea to call local colleges and inquire about their animal programs. Many junior colleges have opportunities you may not know about unless you ask.

7

Working on a Guest Ranch

Horseback trail riding, hay wagons, chuck wagon dinners, hiking, amateur rodeos, and breakfast and twilight rides are just a few of the exciting and enjoyable activities featured at most guest and dude ranches throughout the West. Visitors have an opportunity to live in a setting that is reminiscent of the Old West and to participate in some of the customs of early settlement days.

To keep a guest and dude ranch in operation requires the work and talent of many people, from the manager to the cook, from the ranch hands to the wranglers.

If you would enjoy a summer job during high school or college that would give you a chance to be outdoors, work with horses and people, and enjoy some of the activities mentioned above, then working on a dude ranch may be just what you're looking for. Many ranches hire young people part-time. Others give them full-time summer employment.

Don Monson, manager of The Alisal Ranch in Solvang, California (located near Santa Barbara), loves his work. Although it

Don Monson, manager of The Alisal Ranch, Solvang, California.

is a time-consuming job, sometimes seven days a week, Don says he can't imagine doing anything else. He likes people, he likes to solve problems, and he enjoys the variety that his job offers. And aside from his work, Don gets to play an occasional game of golf when he has a few spare hours.

"Becoming a ranch manager is something you learn from experience," says Don. He began as a bartender and gradually worked into his present job. Although Don has an assistant and many efficient workers in his office, he still deals with many of the situations personally. There is never a boring moment in this work. The Alisal is a complete vacation in one spot. "The Ranch has it all" boasts their colorful brochure: golf, swimming, boating, fishing, horseback riding, badminton, volleyball, pool, and croquet.

Don leaves the horseback riding to the head wrangler because his other duties consume most of his time. Although horseback riding is an important activity on the ranch, many of the guests enjoy their stay without ever getting into a saddle. But for those who love riding there is plenty of excitement and an ample supply of well-trained horses.

"Whether you're an experienced horseman or not," says the brochure, "you'll delight in the riding opportunities at The Alisal." There are more than thirty riding trails that wind through the ranch. And experienced wranglers are on hand to guide guests on a variety of planned trail rides, breakfast rides, steak fries and barbecues in the evenings, two-hour morning and afternoon group rides, even moonlit hayrides. They feature a fine string of Western horses with mounts for every level rider,

Bunk house, The Alisal Ranch.

Guest house, The Alisal Ranch.

and private riding lessons are also available for the experienced and inexperienced.

A Day in the Life of a Wrangler

Western movies and television series have greatly influenced our image of the cowboy and wrangler. So often young people see only the glamour attached to the job. In truth, however, there is a lot of just plain hard work involved.

Here is what the wranglers at The Alisal have to say about the life of a wrangler. Joe Carr, head wrangler, told me that he has been around horses most of his life. He was raised on a ranch in Northern California and has spent over thirty years working with horses in some way or another. "About eight years ago I came through here and stopped for lunch," said Joe. "I filled out an application for a job, but they didn't need anyone at the time. So I headed for San Diego. On my way back from a rodeo one day, the manager called and offered me the job. I've been here ever since. That was 1970."

Joe and the other wranglers spend most of their hours caring for the horses and the guest riders. Joe said they divide the riders into several groups: beginners, intermediate, more experienced, and advanced. There is some loafing for those who want to take it slow and easy, and loping for those who enjoy a bit of excitement. With ten thousand acres of rolling hills on the ranch, there seems to be plenty of variety to suit everyone's tastes and abilities.

Ross Alexander is another wrangler on the ranch. He's been around for five years. He generally works winters at The Alisal and returns to his home in Wyoming each summer. "We have seventy-two head of horses to feed, care for, and saddle each day," said Ross. "We're not too busy right now," he added, looking around the barn, "but come Christmas or Easter and we'll be using all the horses."

Slim and friendly, Richard Silva spoke next. "You have to have patience for this kind of work," he said. "And if you don't like people, don't even try to get into it. Most anyone can learn to ride a horse, but dealing with people is what this work is about, more than half of it, definitely," he added.

"Just about every day something funny or horrible happens. Sometimes it's a real headache taking people on rides, especially when they don't know much about horses. Everyone wants to lope, and they claim they're advanced riders, but out on the trail you find out they don't know up from down on a horse."

Joe Carr, head wrangler, The Alisal, discusses duties in tack room.

Ross Alexander, ranch hand and wrangler at The Alisal.

Richard feels people have been badly influenced by Western movies. "Everyone wants to run," he said smiling. "The truth is a cowboy very seldom runs his horse. Unless he's chasing cattle." Richard tipped his wide-brimmed hat a moment and then went on. "It may be a headache sometimes," he said, "but it's a good job and it's a way of life for me. I've got my freedom. I like being a cowboy but I feel like we're almost a dying-out breed."

Richard has worked other places, sometimes for more money, but he prefers a place where the working conditions and the horses are better. "It's good here," he said. "We get our wages plus room and board. Which is great. This ranch is a good outfit to work for. We get a vacation about one week the first year and after that you get two weeks paid vacation."

It was obvious that Richard was proud of his life as a cowboy. In fact, he had started writing a book about his life as a wrangler. "I think the cowboy image is fading. I hate to see it too, because I remember a time when I was real proud to be a cowboy. I still am—it's just that everyone who sticks on a cowboy hat and a pair of boots thinks he's a cowboy. The image is fading. But I guess that's why we're all here. We want to keep it going."

The life of a wrangler is somewhat the same as a cowboy's, except that there are no cattle in the daily work of a wrangler.

In the old days of the West, as cowboys took care of the cattle on the long drive, they needed someone to drive the extra horses down the trail and take care of them. Hence, the wrangler.

A day wrangler's job begins three or four hours before daylight. He rolls out of the sack, pulls on his boots, straps on his spurs, grabs a hot cup of coffee and maybe a hard roll before the work starts.

Wranglers of today are descendants of the wranglers of the Old West. There are two kinds of wranglers: *Horse wrangler—*

Cowboy's coat room, The Alisal Ranch.

responsible for the riding horses in his care and for doctoring all sick and injured horses. He sees to it that all are shod, fed, and in good condition. *Dude wrangler*—responsible for taking care of the ranch horses and the guests at the dude ranch. He needs to care for the people as well as the horses, as far as riding goes.

Left: *Dick Silva, classic cowboy, ponders life of a wrangler.*

Right: *Horse gets a scratch on the nose from visitor, Erin Sweeney, at The Alisal Ranch.*

Present-day wranglers must not only know the horses, they must know the riders too. It's important to a dude ranch to match the guests and horses well. In fact, that's their most important duty. When organizing a ride, the wranglers assume responsibility for everything that goes on from the time the guests mount the horses until they return from the ride. These are some of their duties:

—They bring the horses to the riders.
—They check the saddles for safety.
—They assist the guests in mounting the horses.
—They adjust their stirrups to fit.
—They demonstrate safety in the saddle and use of the reins.

There are also many other chores on the ranch that the guests never see. These include:
- —Cleaning the horses thoroughly.
- —Cleaning the corral.
- —Loading hay for feedings.
- —Repairing faulty saddles and bridles.
- —Unbridling horses after the day's ride.
- —Driving them out to the feedlot for the night.

"It may seem like a lot of hard physical work," said Richard, "but it is a great life and I don't know of any wrangler who has done this for awhile who'd give it up to do anything else."

Richard then talked about his private feelings. "There is something special about being a dude wrangler, about living in

Linda Shoptaw, lady wrangler, The Alisal Ranch. Loves her work and has no problems dealing with the other cowboys.

the country on a large dude ranch like this. At night, instead of all the noise of the city, you have the noise of cattle in the pastures on the ranch. You also have the clear night air around you and the stars so bright they look like you could put out a hand and pull them from the sky. Out in the country like this, there is never any problem going to sleep at night."

A Lady Wrangler's Point of View

Linda Shoptaw, the only female wrangler at The Alisal, spoke next. "I'm a wrangler just like everybody else here," said Linda, looking fit and pretty in her Western jeans. Her feminine nature came through her soft brown eyes and crop of curly hair. "In fact, I started right here on this ranch. My father was foreman of the cattle ranch, so I spent the first ten years of my life here and have been working as a wrangler since July, 1978. I was hired for two weeks at first and then got rehired. I've been here ever since. I do everything everybody else does. And I don't do so bad on those bales of hay," she said with a twinkle in her eyes. "There's no separation just because I'm a woman. I feed and saddle horses, clean stalls, whatever needs to be done."

Linda's first memory of horses goes back to her earliest years. "I remember sitting out here on the grass waiting for my dad to ride by so I could be put up on a horse," she said. "I want to stay right here working with horses and cattle. I don't feel there are many women who can do this job. It takes muscle, hard skin, and you have to be able to take working around *real* cowboys. They can be tough. Many women would get offended."

Linda does not see her job as a case of women's lib. "If you can do the job, great, come out for it," she advises. "But if you can't or you're not really interested in this kind of work, then don't go for it just because you're a woman. You've got to be willing to work. That's all there is to it."

Although Linda was raised on a ranch, she doesn't feel that it's absolutely necessary to have that background if you want to work on a ranch. "I've known some men who have not had any experience as a wrangler or cowboy. They wanted to start from the bottom. They just went ahead and worked at it. They kept quiet and learned by watching others, and they didn't get offended if they were bucked off a horse or if a cowboy laughed at them. The cowboys are really just laughing with you," said Linda. "They've been through the same thing dozens of times themselves. I love working with them. They're just like family to me."

Cowboy and wrangler jobs are available at dude and working

The Flying H Ranch in Paso Robles, California. Two visitors, Jim and Julie Sweeney, take a pony cart ride at the Flying H.

ranches. Most people interested in this work simply drop in at one ranch and another, as drifters, and pick up work when they can. Some stay on for years, such as Joe Carr from The Alisal. Others work a season or two and then move on. Most have grown up in this atmosphere, and come from similar backgrounds on ranches. This work does not require much training in the formal sense, but on-the-job know-how which comes from actually doing it. Working wranglers suggest kids start by just inquiring, looking at what is available, applying for work, and talking to others already on the job.

A Working/Guest Ranch

Some ranches, such as the Flying H Western Guest Ranch near Paso Robles, California, serve two purposes. They host guests and breed and raise horses and cattle too. The Flying H "is a real working horse and cattle ranch run by three generations of our family," say Gordon and Arline Heath, hosts and owners of the ranch. Visitors have an opportunity to enjoy a peaceful relaxing vacation in the oak-covered rolling hills of the valley next to Lake Nacimiento. At the same time they can see the workings of a real ranch featuring purebred Black Angus cattle, beautiful Arabian horses, big gentle Belgian draft horses, and various other ranch animals.

The White Stallion Ranch in Tucson, Arizona, is another guest ranch that has the spirit of the good old days. Situated in the desert, the four-thousand-acre spread has everything a guest could expect from a visit to the Southwest. Rodeos twice a week, cookouts, barrel racing, fast and slow rides to suit everyone's tastes, cozy cottages, and good home cooking are just part of the fare. In addition to the activities for guests, the ranch also specializes in raising and training quarter horses.

Opportunities for work as a kitchen or dining room helper, housekeeper, ranch hand, wrangler, or office worker are usually available during the high visitor's season at most ranches of this type. Openings, of course, are subject to individual ranch requirements. The best way to inquire is to contact a nearby travel agent or the automobile club in your city or community for a list of guest or dude ranches. Then write to several and request employment information. The summer vacation period is usually the best time to find work part-time. You might begin looking several months ahead of that time.

8

Retail Sales

Owning or managing a tack shop or saddlery is another interesting facet of the horse business. Bill Van Gieson, owner of the Calabasas Saddlery in Los Angeles County, California, talked with interest about his work. "I like what we do here, the equipment and the people, and I love horses," he said. His eyes were friendly and direct when he spoke.

"I owned horses," said Bill, "so I've been around them for several years. Actually I'm an engineer by trade."

Bill and a friend looked for a new business to go into when things in the aerospace industry began to fade. They hadn't been involved in retail sales before but a tack and saddle shop appealed to them. "We've tried to keep the store oriented to horse equipment rather than clothes like so many others. We do carry jackets and some English riding clothing, such as hunt coats, breeches, boots and so on, but our main emphasis is on equipment."

To get started in the tack business Bill felt a person would need roughly $75,000 to $100,000 of inventory at first. When you

Bill Van Gieson, owner, The Calabasas Saddlery.

decide which way you're going to lean or what you want to specialize in, you can increase the inventory. Bill also feels it's easier to buy a shop already in business than to start one of your own. The location is solid and the customers are established.

Bill finds his work enjoyable but he was quick to admit that it requires long hours—ten hours a day, six days a week, minimum. "I try to sneak off every summer for two or three weeks of

Boots are big business at The Calabasas Saddlery.

vacation," he added. "I don't really think there are any disadvantages in the retail business," said Bill. "To me it's fun. You have to like people, though, to stay in this field."

Bill hires students as part-time employees. Many of them own their own horses, are taking animal husbandry or studying veterinary medicine. And most are accomplished riders, either English or Western. He feels their knowledge and experience add to the atmosphere of his store. The students know enough about riding and equipment that they can assist any customer with their needs.

"We don't have a training program. We just show our people where everything is located. Sometimes I get lost myself," he said with a grin.

Young girls seem to be Bill's most enthusiastic and frequent customers. Girls and horses just naturally go together. "We sell a lot of riding clothes and equipment to little girls in the neighborhood as they outgrow what they have."

Calabasas Saddlery is apparently in an ideal location. "We are uniquely situated here," said Bill. "The main thrust of the population is going west. We're right in the path as people go through and we're surrounded by two of the finest riding schools in this area."

Bill and his partner feel fortunate that they found a shop in such a good locale. Location is all important for retail sales. If you want to start a store from the ground up Bill feels that finding a suitable spot "would be a study in itself. You'd need to ask yourself where the stables are, what the needs of the horse community are, is the predominance Western or English, and what the horse population is."

It would also be a good idea to go to the various riding schools and clubs to let them know you are planning a tack shop, to get acquainted, and to become familiar with their needs. Calabasas Saddlery prides itself on knowing its customers intimately. "We call most people by their first name when they come in," said Bill, "certainly our regular customers, at least."

It seems apparent that people in retail sales in the horse industry just naturally love horses and horse people. They enjoy their merchandise and take pride in making the best possible equipment and service available to their customers. The hours may be long and some of the problems frustrating, but like Bill Van Gieson, if you can say with a big smile, "I like what we're doing and I like horses and people," then chances are you'll make it in a tack and saddle shop.

9

Horse Healers and Helpers

Dr. Robert Miller is a lively, talkative, and very mobile man. Each morning he's seen zipping in and out of the office and treatment rooms at Canejo Valley Veterinary Clinic in Thousand Oaks, California, getting ready for his rounds in the field.

Dr. Miller is an Equine Practitioner—a doctor of veterinary medicine who specializes in treating horses. In fact, 99 percent of his practice involves registered and show horses. He has quarter horses of his own.

"Being a vet," said Dr. Miller, "is a very stressful operation. Certainly never a boring one," he added while signing some papers with one hand and dialing the phone with the other.

Dr. Miller received his DVM degree in 1956 from Colorado State University. The training for all vets is the same. At one time Dr. Miller divided his practice between large and small animals. Specialties usually come after some experience in the field. After Dr. Miller's practice expanded, he began to specialize in equine medicine.

"To become a veterinarian it's important to have prevet ex-

Dr. Robert Miller, equine practitioner, making morning calls.

perience," said Dr. Miller, as he led us to his pickup truck outdoors—a well-equipped veterinary clinic on wheels.

"The horse is unquestionably the most dangerous animal I've ever worked with. They are highly athletic, flighty, and fearful creatures," he added. "Being around them while one is growing up is valuable for anyone who wants to practice equine medicine."

Dr. Miller got his experience by working on ranches as a wrangler, a ranch hand, and a horse breaker. He found that he liked horses and people and enjoyed the outdoors. He began practicing veterinary medicine about twenty-three years ago and has spent the last twenty-two at his present address.

"I went to vet school with the idea of becoming an equine practitioner. Being around horses most of my life probably influenced that choice." And Dr. Miller sees great benefits for any young person who works with horses. "It teaches self-reliance, responsibility, and build one's character."

A Day in the Life of a Veterinarian

I made the rounds with Dr. Miller one morning and was fascinated with what I saw. The day started in his office where Dr. Miller treated a cat in between an interview with me, photographs, phone calls, and paper work. About 10:00 he pulled on his coveralls, grabbed his cap, and we piled into his truck and took off for Canoga Park, his first stop. We visited a ranch and breeding farm where Dr. Miller and his assistant, Kim Angell, did a tube worming on a young mare. Next we drove to Hidden Hills and I watched Dr. Miller check a horse for a suspected pregnancy. But it turned out to be a false alarm. Afterwards, Dr. Miller discussed some procedures with the owner, cleaned up at his mobile clinic, and went on to Thousand Oaks for more routine stops. But it was not to be an ordinary day after all. There was an emergency call en route so Dr. Miller and Kim shot over to a ranch on their way back to the office to attend to a horse that was near death.

This is just one day. There are hundreds of others like it and unlike it all during the year. Equine medicine is not predictable, nor is it without pressure. Because of the returning popularity of the horse, many people see the profession as one of glamour and monetary rewards. What they often overlook, however, is the time and cost—seven or more years for a DVM degree, including undergraduate studies—and still more years if one wants to specialize in surgery, radiology, nutrition, and so on. It is a continuing education program. For all equine vets it is also a high-risk occupation involving thousands of miles of travel each year, often over difficult roads and through hazardous traffic, to work with one of the most dangerous domestic animals. In spite of all precautions, veterinarians are still subject to serious injury. All of this requires costly personal and professional insurance.

Long working hours, night calls, continuing pressure, and high operating costs with no fringe benefits add to the stress. And the income is not compatible with the demands. Equine vets often earn less than other professions where the working conditions are safe and the benefits paid for by the company.

Many quit their careers because of these situations. Others continue to practice because the rewards are still greater. They

Dr. Miller on the job.

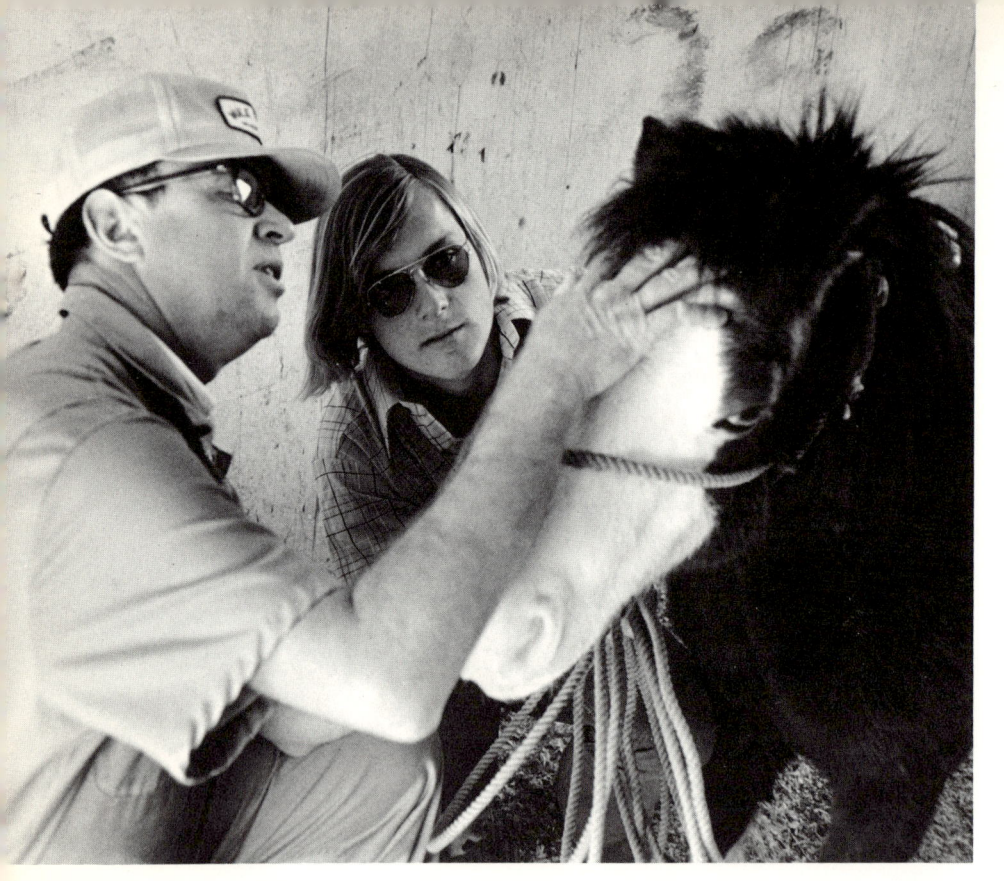

Dr. Miller and assistant, Kim Angell, examine pony for eye disorder.

love horses, people, and the variety and challenge the job offers. Dr. Miller is one of them. "I am happy with my life," he said with a satisfied smile.

Is There a Future for Equine Vets?

Demand for equine practitioners varies with the horse population. Just seven years ago there was a great shortage in the profession. Recently, however, there has been an equally great influx of equine vets and by 1990 the field is expected to be saturated.

"The horse population explosion is an expression of our

affluence and standard of living," said Dr. Miller. "During good times there are more horses because they become a hobby for most owners."

To serve the horse industry, equine practitioners are located throughout the United States. Many operate and maintain modern veterinary hospitals designed specifically for equine patients. Others work as resident vets on breeding farms or racetracks. And still others set up private practices and serve their communities by making the rounds in specially fitted trucks such as Dr. Miller's. They not only treat horses but also act as consultants and advisors in matters of preventive medicine and management.

Although jobs for equine practitioners are getting more scarce as years go on, there is always room for excellence in this field, as in any other. New horses are born every minute, new people come into the business of buying and raising young horses, and new riders climb into the saddle for the first time every year. Therefore, the demand for good quality medical care and treatment will not disappear. A new crop of equine veterinarians will continue to graduate and establish practices across our country. *You* could be one of them!

Large Animal Assistant

Kim Angell is Dr. Miller's assistant and has the distinction of being a first in his profession. Kim filled a job vacated by his brother a few years ago. "My job consists of maintaining the vehicles and keeping them ready for rounds, maintaining the drug and equipment supply, and setting up appointments and checking on past patients. The vets needed assistance with these things," Kim pointed out, "and my duties now free up to four hours a day for them." Dr. Miller and his associates have more time, as a result of hiring Kim, to focus on treatment and preventive medicine, while Kim handles the details of running a smooth business.

In the field, Kim restrains the horses while Dr. Miller treats or examines them; he prepares any necessary drugs or medication, and handles surgical supplies. On some occasions, Kim and Dr. Miller must perform surgery on the spot. This is referred to as "barnyard surgery" because it takes place "in the field."

"I've learned a lot about horses and people since taking this job," said Kim. "Horses are intelligent, sensitive creatures, and those who work with them must have the same qualities. They will respond to whatever mood you create."

Kim gave an example from his own experience. At one time Kim worked with one horse that was very aggressive and stubborn. "I was scared and showed it," said Kim. "Then I realized the horse sensed my apprehension and took advantage of it." From that point on Kim was aware of how his own reaction to the horse triggers a related response.

"A horse will treat you like another horse," said Kim. "It's important as an assistant to be consistent. You need to be firm and deliberate in treatment. You must talk and correct it instantly—but with love."

Veterinary assistants cannot look forward to a large income but they can make a decent living, and for many, the variety, pace, and challenge of the work is more than enough compensation.

Kim also recommends his kind of work as an excellent general preparation for other related jobs. He feels that his background with Dr. Miller has been an education as well as a career. "What I've learned in this work I can apply to any phase of the horse business—drug sales, tack shop ownership, retail sales, ranch management, and so on."

In addition to veterinarians and assistants there are many related careers on the business side of equine medicine. Office workers, clerks, secretaries, receptionists, surgical assistants, and others. Contact a veterinary clinic near you for more information about these jobs or write for details to:

>American Association of Equine Practitioners
>14 Hillcrest
>Route 5
>Golden, Colorado 80401

10

Rodeo Riders

"Rodeo is an original American sport gaining in popularity each year," according to The Professional Rodeo Cowboys Association. In 1978, for example, there were 618 sanctioned rodeos. They drew 16.5 million paying customers and distributed $7.2 million in prize money. In the last twenty years, rodeo has become a big business—a major national way of life.

For the competitor it is a bruising and exhausting life-style which involves thousands of miles of travel each year, too little sleep, and constant physical abuse. Those in the profession, however, seem to recognize its demands and take a certain pride in their own ability, stamina, and the challenge that the work provides.

Tom Ferguson is one of them. Tom, handsome, dark-haired, in his mid-twenties, is a champion—one of the most brilliant of the modern-day cowboys. In fact, he's the first in history to earn more than $100,000 in twelve months. And he has done that for the past three years.

Tom grew up in St. Martin, California, with his brother

Larry, who is also a top steer wrestler and roper, and his parents. Tom's dad had been a rodeo man in the early days, so his sons took to the sport naturally. Tom began roping eight calves a night when he was in high school, and competed with other teenage cowboys throughout the 1960s. He became the amateur (or California Cowboy Association) calf-roping champion as a senior in high school and won a scholarship to the California Polytechnic Institute at San Luis Obispo, California. Today he is the most recognized rodeo hero.

Getting Started in Rodeo

Many of today's college cowboys and many professionals, as well, have been performing since they were eight or ten years of age. They came up from the ranks of the National Little Britches Rodeo Association which was organized in 1961. This organization has sixteen thousand boys and girls from eight to eighteen involved in little rodeos of their own. There are junior and senior divisions for boys and girls and from five to six separate events for each of these categories.

There are also a number of rodeo clinics sponsored and managed by former champions such as the famous Casey Tibbs, rodeo champion of the 1950s. Tibbs was a legend in his top days. He made headlines and lent the sport a kind of glamour it had not had before. His influence reached young and old alike and sparked a rodeo craze that resulted in student rodeo clubs and rodeo programs in more than fifty Western colleges. For a time, Casey, too, ran a rodeo school for young people.

Roy Cooper, twenty-two, is typical of the increasing number of college-educated young men now making a business of rodeo competition. He has been more successful than most, however, earning over $100,000 during his first two years as a professional.

Although most competitors must enter about a hundred rodeos a year in order to make any real money, Roy has proven that you can make a good living if you have a head for the business side as well. Many riders can't keep their minds on roping and wrestling and manage their financial affairs at the same time. They get into a habit of trying to pay yesterday's bills with tomorrow's winnings. But that needn't be the case for everyone or anyone. In fact, there are a number of college courses now that combine book knowledge with practical skills. Sean Davis is one man who operates a college rodeo school within the University of Southeastern Idaho, where he teaches rodeo as an accredited college class.

Girls Go for It Too

Now in action is the Girls Rodeo Association, which was formed in 1948 to meet the special needs of female rodeo participants. Acceptance from rodeo men has not come quickly or easily. "The cowboys put up with us probably because the audiences like us," says female champ, Rosie Webb. "We add a little glamour to the sport." And a little excitement too! Cowgirl Sue Pirtle Hayes rode a bucking horse while eight months pregnant during a recent world's championship show.

Rosie's specialty is barrel racing—a strictly female event. It's a contest of woman and horse against the clock. The rider and mount race from behind a starting line through a cloverleaf pattern around three barrels. The standard course is 60 feet from the scoreline to the first barrel; 90 feet between the first and second barrels; 105 feet to the third; 165 feet back to the scoreline.

Rosie, who came to California to become an actress, found herself involved with horses through a friend. After her first

Barrel racing is a strictly female event.

introduction to rodeo life, she became a part of it in 1963 and has been riding or training horses ever since.

At the beginning of her career she traveled the weekend rodeo circuit in California, Nevada, Arizona, and Texas, often driving one to two thousand miles from Friday night through Sunday.

"I discovered that first year, however, that I needed some help and had to learn to ride better than I did, so I backed off for a couple of years," she said. "I studied films, other girls' performances, and I really worked hard."

By 1965 Mrs. Webb was competing in thirty or forty rodeos a season, trying to catch up with women who had done it all their lives. In 1968 she won top place in California and went on to the

National Finals held each December in Oklahoma City. There she placed tenth.

Since 1970 Rosie has trained barrel horses for other women and given clinics in barrel racing. "If you travel all year and you have a good horse, you can make some money. But it's a job. The competition is getting tough. And it gets very tiring driving all night. I'd say probably the best way to make money in this sport is to stay in your backyard and train and sell horses," said Rosie, who now does just that.

The Ingredients of a Rodeo

The sport came out of the great cattle drives of a hundred years ago when bronc riding and roping contests provided the only entertainment for cowboys during their long drives. It remained unorganized until 1936 when cowboys struck for higher prize money and formed a professional organization.

Every PRCA-sanctioned rodeo has five standard events: three bucking or "rough-stock" contests and two timed events.

Bareback bronc riding is usually the first event. This requires cowboys with strong arms and a keen sense of balance. They ride with one hand holding onto a "riggin'," a thick leather surcingle fitting over the horses' withers, with a leather "handhold" attached. The horses are free to jump and kick, sometimes spin, and the cowboys try to lean back and maintain a spurring rhythm along the animals' neck and shoulders, raking the legs up and down with dull spurs. This is an eight-second event. Cowboys have eight seconds from the time the animals leave the chutes to demonstrate their skills.

Two cowboy judges score the bucking events. Each one watches from the side of the arena to see how well the cowboy rides and how well the animals buck.

Heather Bender barrel racing with her horse, Sunny.

Saddle bronc riding requires a special saddle called the bronc saddle. This event is the cornerstone of rodeo—a classic—and men who compete in it have solid backgrounds in breaking colts. To stay in the saddle requires brute strength, balance, and timing.

Bull riding is usually the last event at rodeos. It is considered the most dangerous by many and certainly the most exciting of all sports events. The odds are overwhelming. A cowboy weighing about 150 pounds pits himself against a bull that weighs close to a ton. The cowboy attempts to ride the animal with one hand firmly attached to a rope encircling the bull behind his shoulders.

Two timed events are calf roping and steer wrestling, and the object in both is simple—to get the fastest time and win first place prize money. In calf roping, cowboys mount fast, well-trained quarter horses. Man and horse work as a team. The goal is to rope the running calf as it starts ahead from the chute.

To be successful, the cowboy has got to be good with a rope. Half the credit for a smooth run also goes to the horse. A good horse will stand quietly, but he keeps his eyes on the calf. When everything is right, the contestant nods his head, the gate opens, and the calf bolts from the chute. Then the horse jumps into high gear in only a few strides to overtake the calf.

Consistency is the key to a good roping horse. A horse that takes one step forward one day and a step backward the next will keep a roper broke and frustrated. The cowboy has to know exactly what to expect.

Steer wrestling, like bareback and bull riding, is an event created strictly for rodeo. It has no ranch background. Again the horse is a big part of the event. The object is for the cowboy to jump off the horse while it is running wide open, grab a running steer by the horns, and twist him on his side.

Team roping is an extra event seen at many rodeos. It's a timed contest. Two cowboys mounted on horses try to throw a loop around a steer's horns and another loop around his heels. When the steer is caught on both ends, with the two ropers pulled back facing each other, time is called.

In all rodeo events there is an element of chance. Cowboys don't get to choose which horses or bulls, calves or steers they compete on. Some animals are going to be easier for winning than others. That's rodeo!

Rodeo Clowns

One sports commentator referred to the rodeo clown as "the protector of the cowboy, the entertainer of the crowd." Although they come in all shapes and sizes, rodeo clowns all have to be top-notch athletes in excellent physical condition. They need to be agile, quick, fearless, and have a thorough knowledge and good memory regarding the bull.

There are two types of clowns—the bullfighter and the barrelman. Both have serious jobs with a touch of comedy. Bullfighting clowns are the track stars. They are put in the arena to distract the bull from the fallen cowboy. If a cowboy has a problem, a clown enters the arena to take the bull's attention off the accident.

The barrelman, on the other hand, uses himself and his barrel as a diversion. He hauls a heavy, battered, but sturdy metal barrel around and folds himself up inside like an accordion. When he's inside he waits for the irate bull to hit him with an unruly horn or hoof.

Rodeo clowns go back as far as 1904 when the well-known Will Rogers appeared at the St. Louis World's Fair as a rodeo clown for a wild west show. Their purpose is to entertain the crowds while there is a lull in the arena action. They come equipped with a collection of trained mules, horses, dogs, monkeys, ducks, skunks, and comical cars. They may also compete as professional cowboys in rodeo events.

According to The Professional Rodeo Cowboys Association, "Clowns are contract members of the PRCA. They are hired by stock contractors and rodeo committees. The clowns are paid a salary but they pay their own expenses. They travel as hard and fast as most cowboys, crisscrossing the country by truck and trailer rather than plane because of their props and miscellaneous acts."

The rodeo clown is a mixture of grease paint, baggy pants, and superb athletic ability. But. most importantly he guards and defends the bull riding cowboy.

People in the rodeo business are in it because they love the life-style. It's exciting, never boring, carefree and challenging, and they get to travel through many geographic areas in a year's time. Although there are some drawbacks—danger, fatigue, and the drastic temperature changes, since most rodeos take place outdoors—cowboys who stick to this business put those considerations aside and focus on the rewards.

"A man pays his money to enter, and takes his chances in the arena," states the PRCA. "No one tells him which rodeos to enter; he's his own boss. And he wouldn't want it any other way."

If you'd like to know more about the careers availiable on the rodeo circuit, write to:

      The Professional Rodeo Cowboys Association
      2929 West 19th Avenue
      Denver, Colorado 80204

11

Breeders

Most horse owners, at some time or another, become involved in breeding. There are large breeding farms where you can learn about this specialty from experience on the job, or you can pick it up by reading, observing, and assisting others. Even if you get a job on a breeding farm, you are likely to begin at some level of apprenticeship.

When it comes to high-priced race or show horses there is a great deal to consider when undertaking a breeding program. Naturally, the owners are looking for the best possible foals. Breeding is a real specialty and not something one can learn overnight.

Anyone who enters breeding as a career has the responsible task of selecting a stallion that will produce the desired result. He or she must be a fine judge of a horse's make, shape and action, and also have a considerable knowledge of the bloodlines of the sire's breed or type.

"Mate the best to the best" has always been the basic maxim of the Thoroughbred breeder and it seems to work. Choosing

Visitors Julie and Jim Sweeney on a breeding farm.

the best in other breeds, however, may not be as simple. Very often what appears to be an outstanding individual to one person may not be to another. It can be a matter of personal, and very subjective, opinion.

However, there are some basic guidelines to follow that will give you some idea of what is involved in the life of a breeder.

—Remain as objective as you can.

—Assess the stallion on the basis of temperament, conformation or shape, action, constitution, soundness, and performance.

—Look at his pedigree.

In breeding it is important to find a stallion that has the qualities that your mare lacks, so the foal will hopefully have her good points plus the stallion's.

As a breeder you will need to know about the reproductive systems of both the mare and the stallion, the breeding season for mares, and the best way to select and manage the stud.

A breeder's job does not stop with the breeding itself. Duties continue while the mare is pregnant, during the birth itself, and after birth with the care and maintenance of the offspring. It is a comprehensive and long-term program—one that requires some medical knowledge and a thorough grounding in the anatomy and physiology of the horse.

With the exception of breeding farm professionals, it is not likely that an individual could make a living from breeding. Most owners are involved in other aspects of the horse industry. They do not rely solely on stud fees or the sale of foals for their

Mare and foal on breeding farm.

main income. Some, of course, work in unrelated professions and simply breed and raise horses as a hobby.

The horse farmer, as most other farmers, occupies the position of greatest risk in his industry. He risks the loss of valuable breeding stock from disease, theft, accident. An oversupply of horses in general or that of a particular breed could also force him to sell his horses without profit. This is especially significant if he has a big investment in land, equipment, and buildings.

Sometimes this risk is offset if he has a chance for a high return on an outstanding horse. Selling an outstanding horse and getting high fees for the use of a top-quality sire can also produce great income.

For the hobby breeder, however, the chance to make a lot of money on an individual horse is not likely. This breeder, then, has to rely on the sale of horses for recreation, and use other part-time breeders for stud service income. Being aware of supply and demand in the horse buying market is important to every breeder. Currently, however, there is such a rapid growth of horse-related activities, that most breeders, commercial and hobbyists, won't have a problem with overpopulation. Timing can be critical. And because of this it's important for anyone who wants to get into breeding to get a thorough knowledge of the business and economic side of the picture.

Whichever route you take—commercial or amateur breeding—you're likely to find the business a fascinating one. What could be more rewarding than being responsible for a mating that produced a magnificent new foal?

12

More Ways to Learn About and Work with Horses

There are several universities and equestrian schools that offer degrees in management or horsemanship. These unique programs offer students intensive, firsthand study about horses, while teaching them the economics of agriculture at the same time.

The University of Maryland, for example, now has a course called "Horse Farm Management" with the emphasis on *doing* rather than watching. All students (twenty-five seniors) participate in the program by getting involved in basic horse care courses, anatomy and physiology of the horse, and engage in training, foaling, breedings, mini-horse shows, and so on. Some students are interested in careers in this area, others take the courses to lend more value and information to their hobbies with horses.

Here are a few schools you can write to for further information:

School	Courses
Department of Animal Science University of Maryland College Park, Maryland 20742	Inquire about special courses in "Horse Farm Management."
Department of Animal Sciences Washington State University Pullman, Washington 99163	Their program prepares students primarily for using horses in recreational pursuits—it is more hobby oriented than others.
Department of Animal Science University of Kentucky Lexington, Kentucky 40506	Their horse program includes both equitation courses and horse production, management, and training courses.
Horse Program Department of Animal Sciences Colorado State University Fort Collins, Colorado 80523	General equitation program. Students with prior experience before entering the program do best.
Potomac Horse Center Route 3 14211 Quince Orchard Road Gaithersburg, Maryland 20760	Their "Horsemaster Course" graduates students who qualify to teach, train, and manage, with a thorough practical knowledge of all stable management, feeding, shoeing, and minor veterinary ailments. Graduated Horsemasters usually take jobs as managers and assistant managers in riding establishments.
Director of Admissions Meredith Manor Route 1 Waverly, West Virginia 26184	Total curriculum that includes daily preparation for employment in grooming, training, showing, teaching, judging, and management.

There are a number of other careers related to the horse business that are not covered in this book. There seems to be no limit! The following list will give you a few more jobs to consider, the kind of work involved, and a professional organization or lead to contact for further information.

Title	Contact	Description
4-H Agent	National 4-H Service Committee 150 North Wacker Drive Chicago, Illinois 60606	Represents members of 4-H groups in shows and competition.
Journalist	American Horse Council 1700 K Street, N.W. Suite 300 Washington, D.C. 20006 (Send $1.00 for their *Trade Press Directory* listing horse publications.)	Requires background in horses and newspaper and magazine writing experience.
Photographer	Write American Horse Council for more information. (Address above.)	Experience in professional photography and interest and background in horses and horse shows.
Racing Chemist	Association of Official Racing Chemists P.O. Box 770 Seaside, Oregon 97138	Responsible for chemical analysis of blood and urine samples of racehorses to check for illegal drugging before races.
Stamp Collector	*Topical Time* 3306 N. 50th Street Milwaukee, Wisconsin 53216 Write for information on horse stamp collecting. This is a hobby that could work into a career.	Not strictly a profession, as such, but you could make money over a period of time. No experience necessary to start.

115

Title	Contact	Description
State Horse Specialist and Extension Horse Specialist	Write the State University in your state and address your request to the Department of Animal Sciences.	Workers provide a resource for horsemen and women and act as a go-between for the state horse industry and the government.
Stunt Man or Woman	Write to various movie studios for information. Addresses available at your library.	Requires acting and trick riding ability; knowledge of horsemanship.
Track Security	Harness Tracks Security 150 E. 42nd Street New York, New York, 10017	Training in security techniques.
Trick Rider	The Professional Rodeo Cowboys Association 2929 W. 19th Avenue Denver, Colorado 80204	Requires a talent for performing special tricks while riding. Showman's ability.

As you become better acquainted with the horse industry, more and more career opportunities will come up. There are dozens of jobs available in every area—nutrition, preventive medicine, mounted police work, polo playing, and so on.

A good way to keep up with the latest work is to subscribe to a horse publication and read books on various aspects of the industry. Perhaps your overall one best source of information on all aspects of the business is the American Horse Council. For $2.00 you can receive the Horse Industry Directory, which is published by the American Horse Council "to provide a comprehensive listing of trade periodicals, national equine organizations, and government information sources." Information contained in the Directory comes directly from the sources listed, so you are sure to have accurate and up-to-date answers to your questions, and a list of places to contact for the areas you are most interested in pursuing. (AHC address above.)

Whatever you choose to do, working with horses is a rewarding, exciting, and pleasurable way to make a living. Have fun with it too!

Index

Alexander, Ross, 76, 77
Alisal Ranch, The, (Solvang, California), 72–85
American Association of Equine Practitioners, 99
American Farrier's Association, 31
American Horse Council, 13, 115, 116–117
American Horse Shows Association, 48, 50, 52, 53
Angell, Kim, 94, 96, 97–98
Animal trainers, 61–66, 69–71
Arizona, University of, 45
Association of Official Racing Chemists, 115

Barrel racing, 102–104, 105
Beckman, Pete, 19–20, 21, 23, 26, 27, 30
Bender, Heather, 105
Bender, Jud, 9–11
Blacksmiths. *See* Farriers
Breeding, 109–112
Bronc riding, 104, 106
Bull riding, 106

Calabasas Saddlery (Los Angeles County, California), 87–91
Calf roping, 106
California Cowboy Association, 101
California Horse Racing Institute, 32–45
Carr, Joe, 75–76, 85
Chemists, racing, 115
Circus horses, training, 61–71
Clowns, rodeo, 13, 107–108
Colorado State University, 114
Cooper, Roy, 101–102
Cormie, Glenda, 32, 34
Cowboys, 75, 78, 79, 83, 100–108. *See also* Wranglers
Crabtree, Helen Kitner, 51

Davis, Sean, 102
Drivers, harness racing, 43–44
Dude ranch, working on a, 72–86

Equine practitioners, 92–99
Equipment, selling of, 87–91
Exercisers, 38, 40–41

119

Experience, importance of, 14, 17, 26, 27, 28, 30, 35, 40, 55

Farriers, 19–31
Ferguson, Larry, 101
Ferguson, Tom, 10, 100–101
Flying H Western Guest Ranch (Paso Robles, California), 84, 85
4-H agents, 115
Fresquez, Jim and Rita, 32–45

Girls Rodeo Association, 102
Grooms, 13, 41–43, 44
Guest ranch, working on a, 72–86

Harness racing, 43–44
Harness Tracks Security, 116
Hayes, Sue Pirtle, 102
Heath, Arline and Gordon, 85
Herbert, Dorothy, 67–69
Horse Industry Directory, 116
Horse racing business, 32–45
Horse shows, 46–53
Horses
   importance of, 14–17
   training of, 38–40, 42, 54–58, 61–71
Horseshoeing, 19–31

Instruction, riding, 17, 54, 58–60

Jockeys, 13, 32–38, 40, 41
Jockey's Guild, Inc., 45
Journalists, 115
Judges, horse show, 47, 49–52

Kentucky, University of, 114

Liebow, Susan, 32, 34, 38

MacDougall, Corrine, 54–58
Management, horse farm, 113
Manager, show, 52
Maryland, University of, 113, 114
Meredith Manor (Waverly, West Virginia), 114

Miller, Dr. Robert, 10, 92–98
Monson, Don, 72–74

National 4-H Service Committee, 115
National Little Britches Rodeo Association, 101

Officials, show, 47–53

Photographers, 115
Potomac Horse Center (Maryland), 114
Professional Rodeo Cowboys Association (PRCA), 100, 104, 108, 116

Racetrack careers, 32–45
   exercisers, 38, 40–41
   grooms, 13, 41–43, 44
   harness racing drivers, 43–44
   jockeys, 13, 32–38, 40, 41
   trainers, 38–40, 42
Racing chemists, 115
Ranch, working on a, 72–86
Retail sales business, 87–91
Riding horses, training, 54–58
Riding instruction, 17, 54, 58–60
Ringmasters, 51–52
Risdon, Tina, 69–71
Rodeos, 100–108
Rogers, Will, 107
Roping
   calf, 106
   team, 107
Ross, Wally, 61–66, 68, 69
Russell, Sanders, 43

Saddle shop business, 87–91
Schools, list of, 114
Schultz, Durie, 19, 21, 22, 24, 25, 26, 27, 29
Security, track, 116
Shoptaw, Linda, 82–83
Shows, horse, 46–53
Shrimp, Ellie, 35–36, 40–41

Silva, Richard (Dick), 76, 78, 80, 81–82
Specialists, horse, state and extension, 116
Stamp collectors, 115
Steer wrestling, 106–107
Stewards, 48
Stratton, Janet, 14, 17
Stunt men and women, 116
Sweeney, Erin, 81
Sweeney, Jim, 84, 110
Sweeney, Julie, 84, 110

Tack shop business, 87–91
Team roping, 107
Tibbs, Casey, 101
Tools
    farrier's, 22, 23, 25, 29, 30
    groom's, 42–43

Track security, 116
Trainers, horse, 38–40, 42, 54–58, 61–71
Trick riders, 116

United States Trotting Association, The, 44

Van Gieson, Bill, 10, 87–91
Veterinarians, 13, 92–99

Washington State University, 114
Webb, Rosie, 102–104
White Stallion Ranch (Tucson, Arizona), 85
Women, careers for, 13
Wranglers, 75–86. *See also* Cowboys
Wrestling, steer, 106–107